THE
WINE LOVER
COOKS

TONY ASPLER & KATHLEEN SLOAN

MACMILLAN CANADA

TORONTO

I dedicate this book to my beloved Tosh…
Who fills my glass with his wine,
And my life with his love…
— Kathleen Sloan

In memory of Stephanie, who loved food and wine.
— Tony Aspler

Canadian Cataloguing in Publication Data
Aspler, Tony, 1939-
The wine lover cooks

Includes index.
ISBN 0-7715-7660-9

1. Cookery. 2. Wine and wine making. I. Sloan, Kathleen. II. Title.

TX714.A863 1999   641.5   C99-931495-5

Cover and interior design: Tania Craan
Cover photograph: Vince Noguchi
Food styling: Julie Aldis
Front inside Chardonnay and Merlot wine labels courtesy of Chateau Ste. Michelle, Woodinville, WA

This book is available at special discounts for bulk purchases by your group of organization for sales promotions, premiums, fundraising and seminars. For details, contact: CDG Books Canada, Special Sales Department, 99 Yorkville Avenue, Suite 400, Toronto, ON M5R 3K5. Tel: 416-963-8830.

We acknowledge the financial support of the Government of Canada through the Book Publishing Industry Development Program for our publishing activities.

Macmillan Canada
An imprint of CDG Books Canada Inc.
Toronto

   2 3 4 5 TRI 03 02 01 00 99

Printed in Canada

Recipe shown in cover photo is Steak on Ciabatta with Stilton Butter Frisée, p. 84.

TABLE OF CONTENTS

INTRODUCTION *vii*

Wine and Food Matching *viii*
Cooking with Wine *ix*

WINE AND CHEESE *xi*

HERBS, SPICE AND WINE *xv*

CHAPTER 1
CHARDONNAY *1*

Sweet Corn and Pepper Chowder *3*
Brandade with Grilled Pita *4*
Cold Cream of Sorrel Soup with
   Smoked Salmon *6*
Salt and Pepper Oysters *7*
Stuffed Swordfish Rolls *8*
Real Crab Cakes *9*
Baked Macaroni with Cauliflower *10*
Warm Salmon Salad with Tomato
   Vinaigrette *12*

CHAPTER 2
CHENIN BLANC *13*

Pistachio Crusted Halibut *15*
Salmon with Cabbage and Leeks
   in Cream *16*
Scallops and Fettucine with Chives *18*
Fritto Misto *19*
Fresh Mushroom Salad with Parmigiano
   Reggiano *20*

CHAPTER 3
GEWÜRZTRAMINER *21*

Toasted Pasta with Scallops and
   Smoked Salmon *23*
Potato Pancakes with Back Bacon,
   Chèvre and McIntosh Apples *24*
Pork Tenderloin with Watercress *25*
Shahi Chicken *26*
Smoked Salmon and Leeks with
   Tagliolini *28*
Haddock in Curry Cream *29*
Lime Ginger Chicken with
   Fresh Salsa *30*
Guinea Hen Korma *32*

CHAPTER 4
MUSCAT *33*

Szechwan Spicy Noodles *35*
Thai Chicken with Holy Basil and
  Red Peppers *36*
Lamb Curry with Apricots *37*
Mum's Lemon Loaf Cake with Warmed
  Marmalade and Crème Fraîche *38*

CHAPTER 5
PINOT BLANC *41*

Kedgeree *43*
Risotto with Butternut Squash *44*
French Onion Tart *45*
Huevos Rancheros *46*
Frittata with Swiss Chard and
  Pancetta *47*
Spanish Bouillabaisse *48*
Cold Chicken Breasts with Tomato Basil
  Vinaigrette *50*
Cod Provençal *52*

CHAPTER 6
PINOT GRIS/
PINOT GRIGIO *53*

Cream of Wild Mushroom Soup *55*
Pesto Crepes with Grilled Swordfish *56*
Mussel Soup with Cream and Garlic *58*
Grilled Veal Chops with Peach Salsa *59*
Sage and Garlic Pork with Apricot
  Chutney *60*

CHAPTER 7
RIESLING *61*

Five-Spice Orange Pork Tenderloin *63*
Grilled Citrus Tuna *64*

Sambal Goreng *65*
Smoked Turkey Tostadas with Salsa
  Cruda *66*
Cracked Crab and Honeydew Melon
  Salad *68*

CHAPTER 8
SAUVIGNON BLANC *69*

Savoury Fritters *71*
Vegetable Terrine with Mozzarella *72*
Orzo with Black Olives, Sun-Dried
  Tomatoes and Chèvre *74*
Oyster Jim's Clayoquot Roasting
  Oysters with Chèvre and Basil *75*
Artichoke and Cheddar Squares *76*
Cannellini Bean and Roasted Garlic
  Salad *77*
Sky-High Quiche with Gruyère and
  Ham *78*
Tarragon Chicken with Cream *79*
Provençal Scallops with Endive *80*

CHAPTER 9
CABERNET SAUVIGNON *81*

Chicken with Red Peppers and Roasted
  Garlic *83*
Steak on Ciabatta with Stilton Butter
  and Frisée *84*
Spicy Sparerib Stew *86*
Linguine with Fava Beans *87*
English Cottage Pie *88*
Sausages and Onions in Red Wine *89*
Bollito Misto with Salsa Verde *90*
Moussaka *92*
Bistro Steaks with Mustard Cream *94*

CHAPTER 10
PINOT NOIR *95*

Grilled Portobello Mushrooms on
    Arugula *97*
Porcini and Sausage Risotto *98*
Pork Loin al Latte *99*
Stuffed Pork Chops with Mushroom
    Cream Gravy *100*
Chicken Breasts with Truffle and
    Fontina *102*

CHAPTER 11
SHIRAZ/SYRAH *103*

Eigensinn Farm Braised
    Beef Shank *105*
Moroccan Lentil Soup Couillard *106*
Venison Agrodolce *107*
Tourtière with Red Onion Confit *108*
Grilled Lamb Tenderloin with
    Pepperonata Buchanan *110*
Duck Breast Ragoût *112*

CHAPTER 12
MERLOT *113*

Roasted Black Peppercorn Prime Rib
    with Rosemary and Garlic *115*
Beef Tournedos with Mustard and
    Onion Sauce *116*
Cheese, Bacon and Potato Cake *117*
Calf's Liver with Caramelized
    Onions *118*

CHAPTER 13
NEBBIOLO *119*

Hunter's Rabbit *121*

Beef Tenderloin with Pot au Feu of
    Winter Vegetables and Black Pepper
    and Breadcrumb Sauce Avalon *122*
Torta Rustica *124*
Osso Buco alla Milanese *126*

CHAPTER 14
SANGIOVESE *129*

Oyster Jim's Clayoquot Roasting
    Oysters with Tomato Compôte
    and Parmesan Crust *131*
Polpette di Carne *132*
Bucatini with Fennel and Tomato *133*
Penne with Wild Mushrooms and
    Tomatoes *134*
Eggplant Parmigiana *135*
Roast Tomatoes Gratin *136*

CHAPTER 15
TEMPRANILLO *137*

Chick Peas and Sausage *139*
Paella *140*
Braised Lamb Shanks with
    Oven-Roasted Parsnips *142*
Lamb with Red Wine and
    Rosemary *143*
Oxtails in Tempranillo *144*

CHAPTER 16
ZINFANDEL *147*

Sausage and Rapini *149*
Lamb Stew with Olives *150*
Grilled London Broil *151*
Barbecued Duck Pasta *152*

Prosciutto Pizza Bianca *153*
Southbrook Farm's Chocolate Bread
    Pudding *154*

Ermite Blue Cheese and Walnut Tart
    Olson *166*
Cantaloupe with Prosciutto and
    Port *167*
Zabaglione al Porto *168*

CHAPTER 17
FORTIFIED WINES *155*

SHERRY *155*

Chicken Livers with Sherry and Shallots
    on Crostini *157*
Ajo Blanco Barrenechea *158*
Creamed Sherried Mushrooms on
    Toast *159*
PEI Potato, Broccoli and Leek
    Soup *160*
Bistro-Style Lentil Soup *161*
Almond Cake *162*

PORT *163*

Pears Poached in LBV with Lemon
    and Ginger *165*

CHAPTER 18
ICEWINE *169*

Grilled Pears with Vanilla
    Ice Cream *170*
Fresh Figs with Honey Ricotta *171*
Apple and Almond Tart *172*
Siena Cake *173*

INDEX *174*

INTRODUCTION

This book is not your conventional cookbook. It's dedicated to those food lovers who scan the wine list before they peruse the menu.

In other words, diners who choose their wine first and then match the dish to their selection.

This is not as bizarre as it might seem. Especially if you're cooking at home. Here's a case in point. You repair to your cellar—or the cubby hole under the stairs where you keep a few bottles of wine—and you find you're out of Chardonnay. But you do have some Chilean Sauvignon Blanc, a bottle of Californian white Zinfandel someone brought to your last party and an off-dry Riesling from the Reingau. What should you prepare to go with these wines?

Or better still, your Uncle Louis (doesn't everyone have an Uncle Louis? If not, you should have. It was Uncle Louis who introduced me to fine wine) gave you a bottle of Château Mouton-Rothschild 1986 for your birthday. You feel like opening it for a special dinner party but you're not sure what to serve it with to do it justice. (Short answer: rack of lamb, a marriage made in culinary heaven.)

Think of this book then as a marriage counselling manual: how to effect the most felicitous match between wine and food. Since we're starting with the wine, each chapter is devoted to a specific grape variety and how the wine made from it tastes in various regions. I also offer substitutes. If you don't have Chardonnay, for example, you'll know what style of wine will best stand in for it (for a crisp, light wine such as Chablis, you could opt for Aligoté, Pinot Blanc, Soave, Gavi; and for a full-bodied oaky Chardonnay, you could try Tokay Gris, Viognier, oak-aged Sémillon).

My accomplished chef and collaborator Kathleen Sloan has developed an international collection of recipes that complement wines made from these grape types. The criteria she used were these: the ingredients should be readily available, the dishes should be simple to prepare, the end result should be delicious.

In addition to recipes for individual wine styles, we offer a series of charts to help you put wine together with cheeses and herbs and spices.

WINE AND FOOD MATCHING

Who hasn't heard—and heeded—the homily, "Red wine with meat, white wine with fish"? By following that advice, you miss out on some great taste sensations. For instance, if you react badly to red wine (the tannins in reds can cause headaches in those who are allergic to histamines), does this mean you must forego the pleasure of a glass of wine with a grilled steak? No, you can drink white wine happily with red meat, as long as the wine has enough body to stand up to the meat. And why not red with fish, if the wine has sufficient acidity to cut through the oiliness? One of the great matches is grilled salmon with a lightly chilled young red Burgundy or Beaujolais.

There are no rules when it comes to matching food and wine, only guiding principles. If you keep the following thoughts in mind, you can enjoy a range of wines without wondering if Bacchus is going to suddenly appear at your table and set about beating you with a vine stalk.

- Match the weight of food to the weight of the wine. Delicate dishes = light wines. Full-flavoured dishes = big, powerful wines. Think of two boxers in a ring. If one is a heavyweight and the other a flyweight, there is no contest. The stronger one will soon overpower the other.
- Salty, smoky, oily or buttery foods require wines with good acidity to cleanse and refresh the palate. Example: smoked salmon, which is salty, smoky and oily, needs a white wine with high acid, such as Manzanilla sherry, dry Riesling, Chablis or Brut Champagne.
- If you like meat rare, select a red wine with some tannin. The blood in meat contains iron, and tannin counterbalances the taste and mouth feel. On the other hand, if you prefer your meat well done, opt for wines that have little tannin or are fully mature (Beaujolais or aged reds).
- Dessert wines should always be sweeter than the dessert. If the dessert is sweeter than the wine, it will accentuate the wine's acidity. Fruit-based desserts work best with wine because of the acidity in the fruit.

• For hot or spicy food, select a wine with residual sweetness (examples: off-dry Riesling, semi-sweet Vouvray, blush wines).

• If you're serving more than one wine at a meal, serve lighter wines before more full-bodied, younger before older.

•Don't serve white wines too cold (you can't taste them properly) or red wines too warm (cellar temperature is best, around 52°F/20°C). If red wine is too warm, chill it for 5 to 10 minutes in an ice bucket.

COOKING WITH WINE

Wine is a highly versatile beverage. Apart from its well-documented health benefits, if taken in moderation, it can be consumed between meals, before a meal as an aperitif to set up the appetite, throughout the meal to enhance the flavours of the food and aid digestion, after the meal as a digestif—or in the meal itself.

A splash of wine in the soup or sauce can add that lift of flavour that takes a dish from the ordinary to the sublime. Meat marinated in wine becomes more tender. A pan deglazed with wine creates an interesting gravy or sauce. Wine boiled to half its volume makes an ideal substitute for vinegar in salad dressings where wine is served. Pears poached slowly in red wine (Amarone or Recioto della Valpolicella is best) make a fabulous dessert.

Here are some tips for the use of wine in the kitchen.

• Only use wines in the pan that you would drink in the glass. Why introduce flavours to a dish that you don't like on the palate?

• Heating wine causes the alcohol to evaporate, leaving the flavour of the wine. Reducing by half concentrates the taste and the acidity.

• Reduce wine over a low heat so that the pan does not burn.

• Add wine to the sauce or dish halfway through the preparation. Cooking wine too long makes it lose its flavour. Raw wine adds a harshness to the dish (except in soup).

• The acidity in wine can curdle milk or eggs. Add cooked wine at the end of the preparation. The same for green vegetables—wine's acidity can discolour them and make them tough.

• If a recipe calls for Champagne and you have none, substitute Gewürztraminer and lemon juice.

• Use gutsy, full-flavoured wines in the kitchen, rather than delicate, subtle ones.

• To store the heel of a bottle of wine (what's left over!) for cooking, pour ⅛th of an inch (3 mm) of olive oil to exclude air.
• Use a Riesling in mayonnaise instead of vinegar or lemon juice.
• Moisten stuffing for turkey with wine.
• Use white wine to marinate fish briefly.
• For sauces, use one part of wine to four parts of the other liquid or cream. Do the same for casseroles, stews or soups.
• Add wine to cut the richness of cheese sauces.

THE WINE LOVER COOKS

WINE AND CHEESE

The most felicitous food combination you will ever experience is wine and cheese.

A well-chosen wine flatters cheese and cheese brings out the best in wine. Of all foods, cheese is the perfect companion for wine because of its fat content, which coats the tongue, softening the tannic edge of young reds and mellowing the acidity in fresh whites.

Canadian VQA wines are particularly suited to the cheeses we produce in this country because of their firm structure and lively acidity. The acid in the wine cleanses and refreshes the palate, setting you up for the next mouthful. There is such a diverse range of Canadian cheeses, from delicate cream to rich, aged Cheddar and savoury blue, that there is no single wine that you can choose to match them all.

Half of the joy of wine and cheese is to discover the combination that appeals to your palate.

When matching wine and cheese, keep the following principles in mind:
- First, determine the style of the cheese and the character of the wine. You can opt for either complementary flavours (a crisp, dry white with a buttery, nutty cheese) or a contrasting taste (a sweet, round red with a salty blue).
- White wine rather than red tends to go better with creamy cheeses (such as Brie and Camembert).

Cheeses are classified on how they are made and ripened.

FRESH CHEESES: Usually white in colour, these cheeses are not fermented and are consumed unripened. Their flavour comes from curdling, giving the cheese an acidic flavour. They can be salted or unsalted, and have herb flavouring.
Examples: Canadian cottage, cream cheese, mozzarella, quark, ricotta
Appropriate wine style: dry sparkling or crisp, dry, light-bodied white wines

SOFT CHEESES: These cheeses have a white, bloomy crust, with a soft spreadable butter-coloured paste.
Examples: Canadian Brie, Camembert, Canadian feta
Appropriate wine style: dry white or fruity young reds

SEMI-SOFT CHEESES: This is a large range of products, with cheeses that are firmer than soft cheeses.
Examples: unripened cheeses—bocconcini, mozzarella; interior-ripened—havarti, Monterey Jack, Saint Paulin; surface-ripened—Limberger, Oka
Appropriate wine style: Gamay, Cabernet blends, Pinot Noir; for highly aromatic cheeses, Gewürztraminer

FIRM CHEESES: These usually come in a large cylindrical shape that has been pressed to remove most of the whey.
Examples: interior-ripened—brick, Colby, Cheddar, Edam, Emmental, Gouda, Swiss, Fruilano, provolone, raclette
Appropriate wine styles: dry rosé, medium-bodied, fruity reds

HARD CHEESES: These are cooked and pressed to remove whey, usually undergoing a long ripening period.
Examples: Parmesan, Romano
Appropriate wine styles: young acidic reds, particularly Italian reds

BLUE CHEESES: Cheeses with internal moulds, which can appear either blue or green throughout the paste.
Examples: Ermite blue, blue-veined Camembert
Appropriate wine styles: sweet whites, robust sweet reds, tawny port

CHEESE	WINE STYLE	WINE
Blue (Roquefort)	powerful, gutsy red/sweet white	Baco Noir/Late-Harvest Riesling
Brick (firm)	dry white/rosé/light red	unoaked Chardonnay, rosé/ Gamay, Zweigelt
Brie (soft)	medium-bodied white	Chardonnay, Pinot Blanc
Camembert (soft)	medium red/full white	Cabernet blend/oaked Chardonnay, Viognier
Cheddar (hard, medium)	dry white/full red	Chardonnay/Cabernet Sauvignon
Cheddar (hard, old)	full red	Merlot, Cabernet Franc
Colby (firm)	fruity red	Gamay, Pinot Noir
Cottage (fresh)	sparkling/light white/rosé	dry sparkling/dry Riesling/rosé
Edam (firm)	fruity red	Gamay, Zweigelt
Emmental (firm)	fresh white/light red	Pinot Gris/Gamay
Esrom (semi-hard)	aromatic white, semi-dry/dry red	Select Late-Harvest Gewürztraminer/Cabernet-Merlot
Feta (semi-soft)	crisp whites	Aligoté, Auxerrois
Goat's milk (soft)	dry sparkling/dry white sparkling	Sauvignon Blanc
Gouda (firm)	full white/dry red	Chardonnay/Cabernet Franc
Havarti (semi-soft)	dry white	Sauvignon Blanc, Aligoté
Limberger (semi-soft)	full red/off-dry white	Cabernet Sauvignon/Late-Harvest Riesling
Monterey Jack (semi-soft)	light white, light red	unoaked Chardonnay/Gamay
Mozzarella (semi-soft)	light white	Pinot Gris, Sauvignon Blanc
Munster (semi-soft)	aromatic white	Gewürztraminer, Late-Harvest Riesling
Oka (semi soft)	supple red	Pinot Noir, Merlot
Parmesan (hard)	full red	Baco Noir, Maréchal Foch, Syrah
Smoked cheese (semi-soft)	fruit red	Gamay, Zweigelt, Pinot Noir

HERBS, SPICES
AND WINE

Every cook knows that herbs and spices can radically alter the flavour of a dish. This means that consideration for the wine you choose to complement the meal becomes paramount.

You wouldn't serve the same wine for rack of lamb as you would for lamb curry (I'll bring my own wine if you answered "Yes, I would" to that challenge); the spices should change your red Bordeaux for the rack to a chilled Gewürztraminer or dry Muscat to do battle with the curry for most satisfying results.

You could, of course, take the safe route and serve a dry sparkling wine with everything you put on the table—from chile con carne to Dover sole to corn flakes, but after a steady diet of champagne, bubbles can get up your nose. One of the guiding principles in putting food and wine together is that you look for the strongest flavour on the plate and match your wine to that. With this in mind, I offer the following chart of grape varieties with the herbs and spices they complement. At our home we use an inordinate amount of herbs and spices (we love cilantro, also known as coriander), and from trial and error we have found that the following groupings work the best:

CHARDONNAY: cinnamon, garlic, marjoram, rosemary, saffron, tarragon, thyme

GEWÜRZTRAMINER: cardamom, caraway, clove, cumin (curry powder), fennel, nutmeg

PINOT BLANC: chives, garlic, oregano, parsley, thyme

PINOT GRIS: basil, fennel, saffron, tarragon, thyme

RIESLING: capers, caraway, dill, chives, ginger, sage

SAUVIGNON BLANC: cilantro, ginger, green peppercorn, lemon grass, parsley

CABERNET FRANC: basil, bay leaf, rosemary, savory, thyme

CABERNET SAUVIGNON: bay leaf, rosemary, sage, tarragon, thyme

GAMAY: basil, oregano, sage, white peppercorn

MERLOT: bay leaf, garlic, juniper, rosemary, sage, thyme

PINOT NOIR: basil, chervil, mint, thyme

ZINFANDEL: basil, bay leaf, black peppercorn, mild chile, oregano, paprika

THE WINE LOVER COOKS

CHAPTER 1
CHARDONNAY

Almost a brand name for white wine these days, Chardonnay is as ubiquitous as Cabernet Sauvignon. Easy to grow in cool and warm climates because of its early ripening, it's a forgiving grape that allows the winemaker much latitude— whether to ferment in stainless steel or oak, and whether to age in a barrel or not. Chardonnay is a compliant hussy of a grape. Anyone can grow it, and if you slap enough makeup on it (new oak) and rough it up in the barrel (stir the lees, or sediment), you're going to make a presentable wine; but at its best it can be the most sublime of all white wines.

TASTE PROFILE

The range of Chardonnay's flavours is very broad, depending on the soil and climate in which it is grown and the treatment it is subjected to in the cellar. Flavours can range from tart lemony and green apple in cool northern regions (Chablis, northern Italy) to pineapple and tropical fruits in warm climates (California, Australia). It can be rich, buttery and nutty, with overtones of vanilla, butterscotch, toast and smoke from oak aging. It develops caramel flavours and a deep golden colour when mature. In Burgundy, Chardonnay takes on an intriguing "barnyard" bouquet when it is mature.

SYNONYMS

Pinot Chardonnay, Morillon (Austria), Melon Blanc, Gamay Blanc, Gelber Weissburgunder (Alto Adige), Weisser Clevner (Germany)

BEST EXPRESSION

white Burgundy (Montrachet, Corton-Charlemagne, Meursault); top Californian, Australian Chardonnay

DRIEST

Coteaux Champenois (still Champagne), Chablis, unoaked Northern Italian Chardonnay

MEDIUM STYLE

Côte d'Or, Mâconnais, Northern Italy, Ontario/British Columbia, New York State, Washington/Oregon, New Zealand, South Africa

RICH/FULL-BODIED STYLE

California, Australia, Chile

SUBSTITUTES

crisp and light—Aligoté, Pinot Blanc, Soave; full-bodied—Pinot Gris, Viognier, white Rhône

SWEET CORN AND PEPPER CHOWDER

Serves 6

Vary the fresh peppers in this recipe if you wish—red or orange bell peppers or sweet banana peppers all work well. And if you want to add another dimension of flavour, roast or grill the corn and peppers before proceeding, which would make serving it with an especially oaky California Chardonnay a natural choice.

4 tbsp	butter	50 mL
2	sweet yellow peppers, seeded, chopped	2
6	green onions, trimmed, chopped	6
4 cups	corn, fresh or frozen (thawed)	1 L
1 cup	milk	250 mL
2-½ cups	chicken broth	625 mL
2	medium-sized red-skinned potatoes, diced	2
1 cup	light cream	250 mL
	salt and freshly ground pepper	
½ cup	freshly chopped chervil or parsley	125 mL

1. In a large soup pot, melt butter over medium-high heat. Sauté peppers and onions until softened, 5 to 6 minutes. Set aside.

2. In a blender or food processor, combine 2 cups (500 mL) of the corn with milk and process until corn is relatively smooth. Add sautéed pepper mixture and process just until blended. Pour the contents of the food processor into the large soup pot along with the chicken broth. Add potatoes and remaining corn and bring to a boil. Reduce heat and cook gently until potatoes and corn are tender, about 10 minutes.

3. Add cream, salt and pepper, and simmer gently for 2 to 3 minutes until heated through. Just before serving, stir in the chervil or parsley.

BRANDADE WITH GRILLED PITA

Serves 8

When shopping for salt cod, look for pieces that are not too yellow or otherwise discoloured, and try to pick the thicker sections from the middle of the fish. The soaking time given here is just a guide; some pieces of salt cod may take an extra day to desalinate, so you may want to start the preparation for this dish a couple of days in advance. While this recipe calls for an extra bit of work up front, the results are well worth it for this hugely flavourful appetizer.

1 lb	salt cod, (soaked see method below)	500 g
2-½ cups	milk	625 mL
1	bay leaf	1
2–3	large baking potatoes, peeled (to equal ¾ lb/375 g)	2–3
	salt	
3 cloves	garlic	3 cloves
½ bunch	flat-leaf parsley	½ bunch
6	pita breads, warmed	6
	juice of 1 lemon	
	freshly ground black pepper	
1 cup	extra-virgin olive oil	250 mL

1. To soften and desalinate the salt cod: immerse it in cold water and soak overnight, changing the water two or three times.

2. Break the cod into chunks and place them in large saucepan. Add milk, bay leaf and, if necessary, enough water so the fish is submerged in liquid. Bring to a gentle boil and poach for about 15 minutes until fish is cooked and falls apart easily. Use a slotted spoon to transfer fish to a bowl to cool. When it has cooled, pull off any skin and discard along with any bones. Reserve poaching liquid.

3. Bring another saucepan of water to the boil and cook potatoes with a little salt. When cooked, drain and leave to cool.

4. Peel garlic and smash with the broad side of a chef's knife. Remove stems from parsley and roughly chop leaves.

5. Place the fish and potatoes in the bowl of a food processor. Add garlic, parsley, lemon juice and a little pepper. Process on high while adding about ¼ cup (50 mL) of the reserved poaching liquid. While the processor is still running, slowly add olive oil in a thin stream until mixture has reached a smooth, spreadable consistency. Tear pita breads into quarters. Transfer mixture to a serving dish to serve alongside warm pita breads.

COLD CREAM OF SORREL SOUP
WITH SMOKED SALMON

Serves 6 to 8

Lemon-like sorrel is a perfect counterpoint to smoked salmon in this easy, refreshing soup. Make sure to include the dollop of crème fraîche or yogurt just before serving. Team with a New World Chardonnay.

3 tbsp	unsalted butter	45 mL
1	large white onion, chopped	1
2 cloves	garlic, finely chopped	2 cloves
3	medium-sized baking potatoes, peeled, diced	3
3 cups	tightly packed sorrel leaves	750 mL
2 cups	tightly packed leaf spinach	500 mL
1 tsp	freshly grated nutmeg	5 mL
½ tsp	salt	2 mL
½ tsp	freshly ground black pepper	2 mL
8 cups	chicken stock	2 L
½ lb	smoked salmon, cut into strips and curled into a rosette	250 g
	crème fraîche or thick yogurt for garnish	

1. In a large soup pot, melt butter over medium-high heat. Sauté onion and garlic until softened, about 5 to 6 minutes.

2. Add potatoes, sorrel, spinach, nutmeg, salt, pepper and chicken stock to the pot. Bring to a boil, reduce heat and simmer for just under an hour. Cover partially halfway through cooking time.

3. Using a hand blender, purée soup until smooth (or process in batches in a blender or food processor). Pour into a bowl and refrigerate until well chilled. To serve, ladle into soup plates garnished with a rosette of smoked salmon and a dollop of crème fraîche or thick yogurt.

SALT AND PEPPER OYSTERS

Serves 4 to 6

Chablis is a fine match for these sumptuous oysters with their peppery undertone. Set out a platter of crisp iceberg lettuce leaves alongside a separate serving dish containing the oysters with a couple of small serving forks and let guests help themselves. Alternatively, the oysters could be served on trimmed toast sections or set into warm tart shells.

24	fresh oysters	24
2 tbsp	black peppercorns	25 mL
1 tbsp	Szechwan peppercorns	15 mL
3 cloves	garlic, peeled	3 cloves
½ tsp	salt	2 mL
3 tbsp	extra virgin olive oil	45 mL
	juice of 1 lemon	
24 leaves	iceberg lettuce	24 leaves

1. Shuck the oysters, reserving liquor. Strain the liquor through a sieve lined with cheesecloth. Transfer liquor to a skillet and bring to a gentle boil. If necessary, add water to make ½ cup/125 mL. Add oysters and poach very gently, 2 to 3 minutes.

2. Use a slotted spoon to transfer the poached oysters to a plate, reserving poaching liquid.

3. In a small heavy pan, toast the black and Szechwan peppercorns over medium-high heat just until they begin to smoke. Remove from heat and cool.

4. Using a pestle and mortar, grind the toasted peppercorns with the garlic and salt to a paste. Add some of the oyster liquor and continue to grind together until it is smooth.

5. Add the oil to the remaining oyster liquid and bring to a gentle boil. Add pepper mixture and oysters to the pan. After a few seconds, remove from heat and add lemon juice. Let cool slightly. To serve, place each oyster atop a crisp leaf of lettuce.

STUFFED SWORDFISH ROLLS

Serves 6

A typical Sicilian recipe, the ingredients of which vary slightly from region to region. The resulting fish rolls can be grilled or pan-fried in a little olive oil.

2 lbs	swordfish, boned, cut into thin slices	1 kg
	juice of 1 lemon	
6 oz	provolone, fontina or caciovallo cheese, diced	170 g
4 cloves	garlic, finely chopped	4 cloves
¼ cup	chopped flat-leaf parsley	50 mL
10	basil leaves, chopped	10
3 tbsp	pine nuts	45 mL
2 tbsp	golden raisins	25 mL
2	eggs, beaten	2
¼ cup	dry breadcrumbs	50 mL
	salt and freshly ground black pepper	

1. Place swordfish between sheets of wax paper and pound gently with a kitchen mallet or rolling pin to flatten. Trim each piece to a uniform size; do not discard trimmings. Pour lemon juice over each piece of fish.
2. In a food processor or blender, add the fish trimmings, cheese, garlic, parsley, basil, pine nuts and raisins. Process just until blended.
3. In a mixing bowl, combine the ingredients from the food processor with the eggs, breadcrumbs, salt and pepper. Place a portion of the filling in the centre of each piece of swordfish. Fold in the sides of one piece of fish and then roll it up from the bottom, securing it with a toothpick. Repeat with the remaining pieces of fish.
4. Drizzle with a little olive oil. Cook for about 7 to 8 minutes each side on a grill, beneath a broiler or in a skillet. Serve immediately.

REAL CRAB CAKES

Serves 4

A really good crab cake should contain just enough ingredients to keep body and soul together—these ones fill the bill admirably. Serve on a bed of shredded lettuce with a few drained capers. Tzatziki makes a nice accompaniment in place of tartar sauce.

1	large egg, lightly beaten	1
1 tbsp	mayonnaise	15 mL
1 tsp	Dijon mustard	5 mL
1 tsp	Worcestershire sauce	5 mL
1 tsp (or more)	hot sauce	5 mL (or more)
¼	red onion, finely chopped	¼
1 tbsp	freshly chopped chives	15 mL
1 lb	cooked crabmeat (fresh or frozen), picked over to remove any shell or cartilage and pulled apart into chunks	500 g
½ cup	fresh breadcrumbs	125 mL
	salt and freshly ground black pepper	
2 tbsp	unsalted butter	25 mL
2 tbsp	olive oil	25 mL

1. In a large bowl combine the egg, mayonnaise, mustard, Worcestershire sauce, hot sauce, onion and chives. Add crabmeat and fresh breadcrumbs and salt and pepper to taste. Using a fork, blend ingredients together well.
2. Divide mixture into 8 equal portions. Shape each one into a cake shape about 2 inches (5 cm) in diameter and about ¾ inch (2 cm) thick.
3. In a large skillet, warm half the butter and oil (the olive oil helps to keep the butter from burning) over medium-high heat. Fry half of the crab cakes for about 4 minutes on each side until golden brown on both sides, turning once with a spatula. Repeat with remaining butter, oil and crab cakes. Serve immediately with homemade tartar sauce and fresh lemon wedges.

BAKED MACARONI WITH CAULIFLOWER

Serves 6

Any tube-style pasta can be used for this dish—macaroni, penne, ziti or rigatoni.

1 tsp	salt	5 mL
1	medium-sized cauliflower, trimmed, separated into 1-inch/2.5-cm pieces	1
12 oz	tube pasta	340 g
1 tbsp	butter	15 mL
1	small onion, finely chopped	1
2 tbsp	all-purpose flour	25 mL
1-½ cups	milk	375 mL
½ cup	heavy cream	125 mL
¼ tsp	freshly grated nutmeg	1 mL
	salt and freshly ground pepper	
¼ lb	Italian fontina cheese, grated	125 g
¼ cup	grated pecorino romano	50 mL
¼ cup	dry breadcrumbs	50 mL

1. Preheat oven to 375°F (190°C). Place a large pot of water on to boil. When it is boiling, add salt and cauliflower; blanch cauliflower for 5 minutes. Using a slotted spoon, remove the cauliflower to a sieve. Rinse under cold running water to stop the cooking process. Drain again and set to one side.

2. Make sure the water in the pot is still boiling. Add pasta to the same cooking water and cook until it is tender but firm. Drain pasta in a colander.

3. In a medium-sized saucepan over medium heat, melt the butter. Add onion and cook for about 5 minutes, until onion is softened. Using a whisk, add flour and stir for 2 minutes until flour is cooked.

4. Gradually add milk and cream and keep whisking until mixture is thickened to make a white sauce. Add nutmeg, salt and pepper and bring to a gentle boil. Reduce heat immediately and simmer for 3 to 5 minutes while stirring. Remove from heat.

5. Lightly butter or oil the bottom of an ovenproof dish. Add a layer of a combination of cauliflower and pasta. Then pour over half of the white sauce. Add half the grated fontina cheese. Repeat with a second layer of cauliflower and pasta and the remaining sauce.

6. Top with the remaining grated fontina and pecorino romano cheeses and the breadcrumbs and bake for about 30 minutes or until golden brown.

WARM SALMON SALAD WITH TOMATO VINAIGRETTE

Serves 4

A pound of fresh salmon can go further than you think, as evidenced by this delightful warm salad that is perfect as a first course for a spring lunch.

3 tbsp	extra virgin olive oil	45 mL
2 tbsp	fresh lemon juice	25 mL
1 tsp	Dijon mustard	5 mL
½ tsp	sugar	2 mL
	salt and freshly ground black pepper	
2	large ripe tomatoes, skinned, seeded and finely diced	2
1 cup	very thin green beans, trimmed	250 mL
1 lb	salmon fillet, skinned	500 g
3 tbsp	peanut oil	45 mL
4–5 cups	mixed salad greens	1–1.25 L

1. In a small mixing bowl, whisk together the olive oil, lemon juice, mustard, sugar and salt and pepper to taste. Stir in the diced tomatoes to combine well. Set to one side.

2. Blanch the green beans in boiling, lightly salted water for 5 to 6 minutes until tender but still a little crisp. Remove from the water with a slotted spoon and plunge into cold water for a minute or two. Drain and reserve.

3. Cut the salmon into bite-sized pieces. In a skillet, heat the peanut oil over medium-high heat. Fry salmon pieces for 2 to 3 minutes, turning once or twice, until fish is lightly browned but still retains a moist, slightly under-done centre (or longer if you prefer).

4. Use a slotted spoon to transfer the salmon from the pan to the bowl containing the vinaigrette and gently toss to coat the fish with the dressing. Add beans and gently toss once more.

5. Arrange salad greens on four serving plates. Distribute the salmon and beans evenly among the plates and serve immediately.

CHAPTER 2

CHENIN BLANC

Chenin Blanc is an old, noble variety that, like Riesling, can cover the spectrum of white wines, from tartly dry to honey sweet. It is also capable of great age owing to its high acidity—30 years and more is not uncommon. Its natural home is the Loire valley, where its first recorded planting (in Anjou) was as early as 845 A.D. An early-flowering, late-ripening variety, Chenin Blanc is the grape used for sparkling wines in the Loire. In South Africa it is used to produced fortified wines and spirits.

TASTE PROFILE

In cool climate regions, like the Loire, Chenin Blanc produces tart, full-flavoured wines that taste of quince and apple. In warm vintages the wine takes on an off-dry, honeyed apricot note with a floral bouquet. When attacked by botrytis ("noble rot" that concentrates the sugars and acids), the grapes become rich in sweetness offering honeyed apricot and peach flavours. Grown in warm climates, such as California, this variety makes a rather neutral wine. Next to the Loire, South Africa makes the most representative style of Chenin, from dry to dessert wines.

SYNONYMS

Pineau de la Loire, Steen (South Africa)

BEST EXPRESSION

the dry and off-dry wines of Saumur, Anjou and Touraine; the sweet wines of Coteaux du Layon, particularly Quarts de Chaume and Bonnezeaux; South African Steen

DRIEST

Vouvray, Saumur

OFF-DRY

Vouvray, Coteaux du Layon

SWEET

Bonnezeaux, Quarts de Chaume, Edelkeur

SUBSTITUTES

Northern Italian Pinot Grigio, Aligoté, Auxerrois, Muscadet, Chenin Blanc

PISTACHIO CRUSTED HALIBUT

Serves 4

Swordfish, shark or any other firm-fleshed white fish works very well with this nutty crispy coating of ground pistachios. Serve with sautéed zucchini and mushrooms and basmati rice tossed with fresh chopped parsley.

4	halibut fillets, 6 oz each (150 g each)	4
	salt and freshly ground black pepper	
3–4 tbsp	all-purpose flour	45–60mL
¼ lb	shelled, skinned pistachios	125 g
¼ lb	unsalted butter	125 g
3 slices	white bread, torn into pieces	3 slices
2–3 tbsp	olive oil	25–45 mL

1. Preheat oven to 450°F (230°C). Pat the fillets dry and season with a little salt and pepper. Lightly dust with the flour, shaking off any excess. Set aside.
2. In a food processor, combine the pistachios with the butter and bread until the mixture is smooth. Season to taste and reserve.
3. In a skillet, heat the oil over high heat. Add fish fillets and sauté for 1 minute on each side until slightly brown and flour is cooked. Remove from heat.
4. Spread some pistachio mixture on each fillet. If skillet is ovenproof, use the same pan; otherwise, use a metal spatula to transfer the fillets to an ovenproof pan. Roast the fish for 8 to 10 minutes until the fillets are cooked through and the tops golden brown.
5. Remove from oven and serve as described above.

SALMON WITH CABBAGE AND LEEKS IN CREAM

Serves 4

Be careful not to overcook the cabbage and leeks in this recipe, as their brilliant green colour lends much eye appeal to the finished dish. Elegant, pretty and quite delicious.

½ large head	Savoy cabbage	½ large head
½	large leek	½
	salt	
½ cup	unsalted butter	125 mL
6 tbsp	heavy cream	90 mL
1	shallot, minced	1
¼ cup	dry white wine	50 mL
¼ cup	white wine vinegar	50 mL
	freshly ground white pepper	
1 tbsp	extra virgin olive oil	15 mL
4 (6 oz each)	salmon fillets	4 (150 g each)
2 tbsp	fresh chopped chives	25 mL
1 tbsp	fresh chopped parsley	15 mL

1. Bring a large pot of water to boil. Wash and trim the cabbage; discard core and any tough outer leaves. Using a sharp knife, slice into slivers. Wash and trim the leek; slit it lengthwise and, under running water, wash it well, opening up inner leaves to remove any dirt. Slice into slivers.

2. Add a little salt to the boiling water. Add cabbage and leek and blanch for about 1 minute. Remove with a slotted spoon and drain well. Retain cooking water and leave on a low heat, covered.

3. In a large sauté pan, warm 2 tbsp (25 mL) of the butter. Add cabbage and leek and cook for about 2 to 3 minutes. Season to taste and cook for another 5 minutes; it should still be rather crunchy. Carefully stir in 5 tbsp (75 mL) of the cream and cook gently for another 1 or 2 minutes. Set to one side and keep warm.

4. In a small saucepan, warm 1 tbsp (15 mL) of the butter. Add shallot and a little salt and sauté over low heat for about 3 minutes. Add the wine, vinegar and pepper and bring to a gentle boil. Cook until reduced somewhat, about 2 to 3 minutes. Remove from heat and gradually whisk in the remaining cream and butter. Whisk together gently until smooth and creamy. Correct seasoning. Cover top loosely with wax paper and place pot over the reserved pot of simmering water to keep warm. Cover loosely with lid.

5. Set a large nonstick skillet over medium high heat. Add oil. When skillet is hot, add salmon fillets, skin side down. Cook salmon, without flipping, until skin is nicely crisped, 3 to 4 minutes (longer if you prefer). Carefully turn the salmon to cook for a brief time on the other side (less than 1 minute).

6. Remove the pan from the heat and let salmon rest in the pan. To serve, spoon cabbage and leek mixture into the centre of four plates. Top each with a fillet of salmon; spoon sauce around the cabbage. Sprinkle with chives and parsley and serve immediately.

SCALLOPS AND FETTUCCINE WITH CHIVES

Serves 4

The fresh, crisp qualities of Chenin Blanc make it the perfect partner to this full-flavoured pasta dish. Vary the pasta choice to suit your taste.

For the dressing

¼ cup	extra virgin olive oil	50 mL
2 tbsp	white wine vinegar	25 mL
	salt and pepper	

For the pasta

4 oz	fettuccine	125 g
1	small shallot, finely chopped	1
2 tbsp	Chenin Blanc	25 mL
1 tsp	lemon zest	5 mL
½ cup	heavy cream	125 mL
	salt and pepper	
1 tbsp	olive oil	15 mL
1 lb	fresh scallops	500 g
2 tbsp	chopped fresh chives	25 mL
2	large ripe tomatoes, seeded, diced	2

1. In a small mixing bowl, whisk together the ingredients for the dressing. Reserve.

2. In a large pot of boiling, lightly salted water, cook pasta until just tender. Drain and set aside.

3. In a skillet, combine the shallots, wine, lemon zest and cream. Cook over medium heat until mixture is slightly thickened and reduced somewhat, about 10 minutes. Add reserved pasta and season with salt and pepper. Cover and set aside.

4. In a nonstick skillet, warm oil over medium heat. Quickly sear scallops for about 1 minute on each side until browned. Pour the reserved dressing over the scallops. Add half the chives and stir to combine.

5. Divide pasta between four plates. Place scallops on top of each serving. Garnish with reserved chives and diced tomatoes. Serve immediately.

FRITTO MISTO

Serves 6 to 8

Fritto misto is Italian for a "mixed fry," which can include pieces of vegetable, seafood, fish or cheese. Sections of squid, cod and shrimp are used here, all of which marry well with a well-chilled Chenin Blanc.

2 cups	sifted all-purpose flour	500 mL
1-½ tsp	salt	7 mL
¼ tsp	freshly ground black pepper	1 mL
2 tsp	paprika	10 mL
4	eggs, separated	4
2 cups	lager	500 mL
¼ cup	butter, melted, cooled	50 mL
1 lb	squid, cleaned and cut into pieces	500 g
1 lb	large shrimp, peeled, deveined	500 g
1 lb	cod, cut into chunks	500 g
4 cups	vegetable or peanut oil, for frying	1 L

1. In a mixing bowl, sift together the flour, salt, pepper and paprika.
2. In another mixing bowl, beat the egg yolks until they are light-coloured. Add the lager and combine this mixture with the flour mixture, stirring lightly only until just blended.
3. Stir in the butter. Let stand at room temperature for about 1-½ hours.
4. In a dry mixing bowl, beat the egg whites until stiff, then fold into the batter. In a wok, deep fryer or deep, heavy skillet, heat oil to 375°F (190°C). Dip pieces of squid, shrimp and cod into the batter, shake off excess and immerse in the hot oil. Fry until golden brown, about 2 to 3 minutes.
5. Remove seafood with slotted spoon to a tray lined with paper towel. Sprinkle with a little salt and serve with fresh lemon wedges. (Cooled oil may be poured through a coffee filter into a storage jar, refrigerated and reserved for another occasion.)

FRESH MUSHROOM SALAD WITH PARMIGIANO REGGIANO

Serves 4 to 6

Choose a New Zealand Chenin Blanc, or any other of your choice with good acidity, for this salad that features pristine button mushrooms marinated in a lemony vinaigrette. A serious treat for mushroom lovers.

¼ cup	extra virgin olive oil	50 mL
2 tbsp	lemon juice	25 mL
1 tbsp	Dijon mustard	15 mL
1 tsp	sugar	5 mL
1 tsp	salt	5 mL
	freshly ground black pepper	
4 cups	white button mushrooms, quartered	1 L
¼ cup	chopped flat-leaf parsley	50 mL
10 oz	Parmigiano Reggiano, shaved	300 g

1. In a large bowl, whisk together oil and lemon juice. Whisk in mustard, sugar, salt and black pepper.
2. Add mushrooms and parsley and toss to gently coat. Allow to sit for 1 hour at room temperature before serving. Let the cheese also come to room temperature.
3. To serve, distribute between four and six salad plates and top with slices of Parmigiano Reggiano, a drizzle of oil and a fine grinding of black pepper.

CHAPTER 3

GEWÜRZTRAMINER

The name says it all: *Gewürz* in German means spicy; *Traminer* is German for "of or from the town of Tramin" in the Austrian Tyrol (or Tremeno in the Italian Tyrol), where this highly perfumed grape was first propagated a thousand years ago.

TASTE PROFILE

At its most blatant, Gewürztraminer has a bouquet of lychee nuts and roses, with overtones of red pepper and cabbage leaf when overripe, giving it an oily feel in the mouth. It can range in taste from very dry (although its aromatic fruitiness gives the impression of sweetness on the nose) to off-dry and sweet when harvested late. If its pinkish berries are attacked by botrytis (noble rot), it becomes honeyed and can lose its distinctive flavour and be almost indistinguishable from Riesling.

Although this grape is known as Gewürztraminer in Alsace, its spiritual home, it is commonly referred to as Traminer in the rest of Europe, particularly in eastern European countries such as Hungary and Romania. Generally low in acidity and high in alcohol, it does best in cool growing regions, such as Alsace, Germany, Austria and New Zealand, which allow for greater acidity in the wine. It also makes excellent Icewine in Ontario and British Columbia. Because of the grape's pinkish hue, the resulting wine is usually deeply coloured, especially in warm growing regions such as California, Australia and Chile.

SYNONYMS
Traminer Musqué, Traminer Aromatique, Clevner, Red Traminer

BEST EXPRESSION
Alsace, especially from single vineyard sites in the Haut-Rhin (producers such as Domaine Weinbach, Zind-Humbrecht, Hugel, Trimbach, Josmeyer)

DRIEST
Alto Adige, Austria, Ontario/BC, New York State

MEDIUM SWEET
California, Australia, German Gewürztraminer Spätlese

SWEET
Vendange Tardive and Sélection de Grains Nobles (Alsace), German Gewürztraminer Auslese (and higher sugar levels)

SUBSTITUTES
dry Muscat, off-dry Riesling

THE WINE LOVER COOKS

TOASTED PASTA WITH SCALLOPS AND SMOKED SALMON

Serves 4

Eric Brennan, Executive Chef at the Four Seasons Hotel in Toronto, created this impressive first course. The uniqueness of this dish lies in "toasting" the angel hair pasta in the oven prior to cooking. This simple step lends a whole other textural and flavour quality to the pasta that melds beautifully with the seafood and fresh herbs. If cost is no object, choose the best caviar you can afford to garnish each serving, or omit it.

½ lb	angel hair pasta	250 g
	salt	
½ cup	dry vermouth	125 mL
1 cup	crème fraîche	250 mL
8	fresh sea scallops, thinly sliced	8
¼ lb	smoked salmon	125 g
1 tbsp	fresh chopped dill	15 mL
1 tbsp	fresh chopped chervil	15 mL
1 tbsp	fresh chopped chives	15 mL
4 tbsp	caviar (optional)	60 mL
	freshly ground black pepper	

1. Preheat oven to 350°F (180°C). Place a large pot of water on to boil. Spread angel hair pasta on a baking sheet. Place pasta in the oven to brown, about 5 minutes.
2. Add the pasta and a little salt to the boiling water. Cook until just done. Meanwhile, combine vermouth, crème fraîche and scallops in a heavy-bottomed saucepan. Simmer over medium heat for 2 minutes. Add smoked salmon, dill, chervil and chives, and combine well.
3. Strain and add pasta to contents of the saucepan. Combine together well. Season to taste. Serve in pasta bowls and garnish each serving with a spoonful of caviar and a sprinkling of pepper.

POTATO PANCAKES WITH BACK BACON, CHÈVRE AND MCINTOSH APPLES

Serves 4

This makes a lovely appetizer, one that seems to appeal to everyone's memory of how good and comforting potato pancakes can be. Choose a mild and mellow chèvre for this.

4	thick slices back bacon, cooked and cut into strips	4
1	very large baking potato	1
2	eggs	2
¼ cup	all-purpose flour	50 mL
¼ cup	heavy cream	50 mL
1	shallot, minced	1
	salt and freshly ground pepper	
3 tbsp	unsalted butter	45 mL
2 tbsp	olive oil	25 mL
2	McIntosh apples, peeled, cored, sliced into 8 pieces each (cover with cold water mixed with the juice of half a lemon to prevent browning)	2
½ tsp	cinnamon	2 mL
½ tsp	nutmeg	2 mL
½ lb	chèvre, at room temperature, divided into 12 slices	250 g

1. In a large skillet, fry back bacon until cooked through. Remove from skillet and keep warm.
2. Wash, peel and grate potato. Squeeze out and discard any excess water.
3. In a mixing bowl, whisk together the eggs, flour, cream and shallot. Add grated potato and salt and pepper to taste.
4. In a large skillet, warm half the butter and half the oil over medium heat. When hot, add the potato mixture 2 spoonfuls at a time to form an oval shape. Sauté the pancakes on medium heat until cooked through, turning once or twice, about 8 minutes in total per pancake. Repeat procedure with remaining potato mixture. Keep cooked pancakes warm.

5. Wipe skillet with paper towel. Add remaining butter and oil; when melted, add apple slices. Add cinnamon and nutmeg and stir to coat apples well. Sauté apple slices for a few minutes until they are golden brown and aromatic.

6. Divide the pancakes and apples into four portions. Top pancakes with slices of chèvre and strips of bacon. Serve immediately.

PORK TENDERLOIN WITH WATERCRESS

Serves 6

This is a very simple, yet impressive entrée that can be ready in a short time. Serve with steamed rice tossed with cashews and a little sesame oil. While the amount of watercress may seem excessive, watercress "cooks down" owing to its water content, much like spinach and rapini. In this recipe, light soy sauce does not refer to "lite" soy sauce but rather a variety of soy sauce that is lighter in tone and flavour than the darker sauce.

4 bunches	watercress, washed, drained and stems trimmed	4 bunches
	salted water	
¼ cup	peanut oil	50 mL
2 cloves	garlic, finely chopped	2 cloves
1 lb	pork tenderloin, thinly sliced lengthwise into strips	500 g
8	water chestnuts, thickly sliced	8
¼ cup	light soy sauce	50 mL

1. In a large bowl, cover the watercress in salted water and soak for about 30 minutes.

2. Drain, rinse well in fresh water and pat dry.

3. In a wok or large skillet, heat the oil over high heat. Add garlic and pork and brown the meat quickly on all sides. Add water chestnuts and continue to cook, stirring, for another minute.

4. Add soy sauce and watercress and stir to combine well. Cover with a lid and as soon as steam begins to escape from beneath the lid (which shouldn't take long), stir the contents of the pan again, reduce heat somewhat and replace the lid to cook another 2 minutes. Serve immediately.

SHAHI CHICKEN

Serves 4

For years, this dish has been a mainstay at Sher-E-Punjab, a justifiably popular Indian restaurant situated on the Danforth in the midst of Toronto's Greektown. It is rich in flavour and texture, unmistakably Punjabi in origin and incredibly delicious. If you're serving other Indian-style dishes, this recipe feeds four; otherwise, two can enjoy it on its own.

Garam masala is an Indian spice blend that varies to a great degree according to the chef who puts the various ingredients together. You can find good-quality garam masala (which translates somewhat misleadingly as "hot spices") at East Indian supermarkets and specialty food shops. Or try this relatively classic combination that you can vary according to your preference: 1 tbsp (15 mL) cardamom seeds, 1 tsp (5 mL) whole cloves, 1 tsp (5 mL) whole black peppercorns, 1 tsp (5 mL) whole mustard seeds, 1 tsp (5 mL) whole black cumin seeds, a 2-inch (5 cm) stick of cinnamon and a third of a whole nutmeg. Place all ingredients in a coffee grinder and grind to a fine powder.

½ cup	unsalted cashews	125 mL
3 tbsp	vegetable oil	45 mL
1	onion, finely chopped	1
1 tsp	garam masala	5 mL
2 cloves	garlic, minced	2 cloves
1 tsp	ginger	5 mL
¼ tsp	cayenne	1 mL
¼ tsp	coriander	1 mL
¼ tsp	turmeric	1 mL
1 lb	boneless chicken breasts, cut into 1-inch (2.5-cm) strips	500 g
1-½ cups	canned crushed tomatoes	375 mL
¼ cup	water	50 mL
¼ cup	whipping cream	50 mL
¼ cup	sultana (golden) raisins	50 mL

1. Put cashew nuts in a small bowl and cover with hot water. Soak for ½ hour. Drain all but a little bit of the water, then transfer nuts and reserved water to a blender. Process until a smooth paste forms. Reserve.

2. In a skillet, warm the oil over medium-high heat and sauté the onion until it is pale golden, about 5 minutes. Add half of the garam masala and continue to sauté for 1 or 2 minutes.

3. Add garlic, ginger, cayenne, coriander and turmeric to the pan and cook for another minute or two to allow spices to lose their raw taste. Add chicken strips and toss to coat well with the spices and cook for about 2 minutes.

4. Add tomatoes and water and stir to combine well. Cook at a simmer until chicken is cooked through, about 15 minutes. Add cashew mixture and cream and stir to combine well. Bring mixture to a gentle boil, then reduce heat (if, at this point, the mixture is too thick, add a little more water).

5. When mixture has reached a thick and smooth consistency, add raisins and the remaining garam masala. Serve with steamed basmati rice and a *sambal* (side dish) of thinly sliced white onion tossed with malt vinegar, salt and freshly chopped mint.

SMOKED SALMON AND LEEKS
WITH TAGLIOLINI

Serves 4

Tagliolini are thin ribbon-like noodles. If you cannot obtain this type of pasta easily, use spaghettini, angel hair or any thin, strand-style pasta. Use both the green and white part of the leeks for added colour and flavour.

3 tbsp	butter	45 mL
2	leeks, trimmed, washed and sliced	2
1 cup	chicken broth	250 mL
2 tbsp	Dijon mustard	25 mL
1 cup	heavy cream	250 mL
1 tbsp	lemon zest, finely chopped	15 mL
	salt and freshly ground black pepper	
8 oz	tagliolini	250 g
⅓ lb	smoked salmon, cut into strips	175 g
2 tbsp	fresh chopped dill	25 mL
3 tbsp	capers, drained	45 mL

1. In a large skillet, melt the butter over medium-high heat. Sauté the leeks until they are softened, about 10 minutes. Set to one side and keep warm.
2. In a saucepan, over medium-high heat, combine the chicken broth with the mustard, cream and lemon zest. Whisk together to blend ingredients, reduce heat a little and allow to cook until a sauce-like consistency is reached, about 8 to 10 minutes. Season to taste.
3. Meanwhile, bring a large pot of water to boil. Add pasta, along with a little salt, and cook pasta until tender but firm. Drain well, but don't rinse the cooked pasta.
4. Add the sauce, leeks, salmon, dill and capers to the pasta. Toss gently and serve immediately.

HADDOCK IN CURRY CREAM

Serves 6

This comforting dish makes a very pleasant luncheon or first course choice. Vary it from time to time by using smoked haddock fillets. Use the same wine in the recipe that you plan to serve at the table.

2 lbs	haddock fillets	1 kg
1 cup	water	250 mL
1 cup	white wine	250 mL
½	bay leaf	½
3 tbsp	butter	45 mL
2	shallots, finely chopped	2
1 stalk	celery, finely chopped	1 stalk
1 tbsp	curry powder	15 mL
2 tbsp	all-purpose flour	25 mL
½ cup	white wine	125 mL
	salt and freshly ground white pepper	
2 tbsp	chopped fresh parsley	25 mL

1. Pat the fish fillets dry and place in a large skillet. Cover with the water and wine and add bay leaf. Cover with a lid and simmer over gentle heat for about 10 minutes. Do not allow to boil.

2. Drain the stock from the skillet and reserve.

3. Using a metal spatula, transfer fish fillets to a warmed serving platter and keep warm.

4. In a saucepan, melt the butter over medium heat and sauté the shallots and celery until softened, about 8 minutes. Stir in curry powder and flour and cook, stirring with a whisk for 1 or 2 minutes. Gently incorporate the reserved fish stock into the flour mixture, using the whisk to prevent lumps. Then whisk in the wine and cook until sauce is smooth and thickened.

5. Simmer for about 5 minutes and adjust salt and pepper to taste. Pour the sauce over the fish and sprinkle with chopped parsley. Serve immediately with boiled new potatoes.

LIME GINGER CHICKEN WITH FRESH SALSA

Serves 4 to 6

Lively and bright-tasting, this easy dish relies on the freshness of the individual ingredients to carry it off successfully. When handling fresh chiles, wear rubber gloves and avoid all contact with your face.

4	large boneless, skinless chicken breasts	4
⅓ cup	fresh lime juice	75 mL
2 tsp	fresh, chopped gingerroot	10 mL
3 cloves	garlic, finely chopped	3 cloves
1	small dried red chile	1

For the salsa

½ lb	ripe plum tomatoes, diced	250 g
1	medium green bell pepper, diced	1
1	fresh jalapeño, seeded, diced	1
1	medium-sized red onion, diced	1
2 tbsp	chopped fresh coriander	25 mL
2 tbsp	olive oil	25 mL
	juice of 1 lime	
1 large clove	garlic, minced	1 large clove
1 tsp	hot sauce	5 mL
	salt and freshly ground black pepper	
	juice of 1 lime	
	fresh coriander for garnish	

1. Halve each chicken breast, then slice into 1-inch (2.5-cm) wide strips. Set aside.

2. In a mixing bowl, combine lime juice, gingerroot and garlic. Crush the red chile and add to the bowl. Mix to blend ingredients, then add chicken strips. Toss to coat the chicken with the marinade, cover with plastic wrap and chill for at least 2 hours or overnight.

3. To make the salsa, in a small bowl combine the tomatoes, green pepper, jalapeño, onion, coriander, 1 tbsp (15 mL) of the oil, lime juice, garlic, hot sauce and salt and pepper to taste. Mix to blend well and set to one side.

4. Heat the remaining olive oil in a large skillet over high heat. Add chicken strips and cook quickly until brown on all sides, about 4 to 5 minutes all together. Remove chicken to a warm platter. Deglaze the hot pan with the lime juice and scrape up any bits clinging to it. Bring to a boil, remove from heat and pour over chicken.

5. Serve with fresh salsa and garnish with fresh coriander, and extra lime if you wish.

GUINEA HEN KORMA

Serves 4

A *korma* is a curry that is mild in flavour and generally creamy. In this version, tender guinea hen is combined with a substantial amount of cardamom subdued by the addition of thick yogurt and rich cream. Cornish game hens may be used in place of the guinea hen with good results.

4 tbsp	vegetable oil	50 mL
2-½–3 lb	guinea hen, cut into pieces	1.13–1.5 kg
1	large onion, finely chopped	1
2 clove	garlic, finely chopped	2 cloves
2 tsp	fresh chopped gingerroot	10 mL
1	cinnamon stick, broken	1
8	green cardamom pods, slightly crushed	8
3	cloves	3
1 cup	yogurt	250 mL
	salt and freshly ground white pepper	
3/4 cup	heavy cream	175 mL
3 tbsp	chopped fresh coriander	45 mL

1. In a large, deep casserole or Dutch oven, warm half of the oil over high heat. Brown the pieces of guinea hen a few at a time. Transfer the pieces to a platter. Reduce heat slightly and add remaining oil to the pan.

2. Add onion and sauté for 5 minutes or so until softened and beginning to colour. Add garlic and ginger and continue to sauté. Add cinnamon stick, cardamom and cloves and continue sautéing for about 3 to 4 minutes, stirring continuously.

3. Add the yogurt and stir to combine well, cooking the mixture for about 2 minutes to allow it to thicken. Add pieces of browned guinea hen, salt and pepper and about ¾ cup (175 mL) boiling water. Bring to the boil, reduce heat and let simmer for about 30 minutes, when the meat should be tender.

4. Add cream, stir to incorporate it into the sauce and let simmer for a few more minutes. Adjust seasoning. Sprinkle with coriander and serve with a rice pilau or simply steamed rice.

CHAPTER 4

MUSCAT

Of all grapes, Muscat has the largest family tree and is believed to be the oldest variety known to humankind. The wines mentioned in the Greek epics were probably made from Muscat grapes, and ampelographers—specialists in the study of vines—believe that all the wine grapes we know today are mutations of Muscat varieties. Greek and Roman traders took cuttings and planted them around the Muscat grapes that flourish still on the islands of Samos, Cephalonia and Patras.

There are over 200 different types of Muscat grown around the world, from the palest white-yellow in colour to mourning black. Delicious as table grapes, Muscat in its many forms is the most widely planted grape on the planet. The wine they produce is as near to the taste of the grape as you will get.

TASTE PROFILE

Generally sweet in flavour, Muscat has elements of carnation, cardamom, musk melon and orange blossom on the nose and the palate. Like Gewürztraminer, its bouquet suggests sweetness, although Muscat can be quite dry. The black version (Muscat Hamburg) can have blackcurrant flavours. It can be light and delicate, such as in the still and sparkling wines of Moscato d'Asti in Piedmont (which have as little as 5 per cent alcohol), and it can make the thick and lusciously sensuous liqueur Muscats of Australia, the Greek Islands, the Mediterranean basin. In Chile, Muscat is distilled to produce a local eau de vie called Pisco.

SYNONYMS

Muscat Blanc à Petits Grains, Muscat de Frontignan, Muscat d'Alsace, Muskateller, Muscat Canelli, Moscato d'Asti, Muscat d'Alexandrie

DRIEST

Alsace Muscat, Austrian Muscat

MEDIUM SWEET

Moscato d'Asti, Asti Spumante, Clairette de Die

SWEET

Beaumes de Venise, Frontignan, Banyuls, Rivesaltes, Samos and other Greek
Muscats; Black Muscat—Quady Elysium from California

SUBSTITUTES

dry—Gewürztraminer

SZECHWAN SPICY NOODLES

Serves 4

While many authentic Chinese dishes are a bit ambitious for the home chef, there are a few—such as this one—that can be made easily and quickly with great success. In place of the chicken or pork, you can substitute chunks of tofu to make this a vegetarian dish.

Szechwan peppercorns are often labelled as dried red pepper in Asian markets. They're not actually peppercorns at all, but the dried berries of the Chinese prickly ash tree that contain a tiny seed.

1 pkg	thick Chinese noodles (12-oz pkg/375 g pkg)	1
4	green onions, chopped	4
3 tbsp	chopped fresh coriander	45 mL
2 cloves	garlic, minced	2 cloves
2 tbsp	smooth peanut butter	25 mL
2 tbsp	Chinese chile sauce	25 mL
1 tbsp	light soy sauce	15 mL
1 tbsp	rice wine vinegar	15 mL
1 tbsp	sesame oil	15 mL
2 tbsp	vegetable oil	25 mL
2 tbsp	water	25 mL
10–12	Szechwan peppercorns, toasted	10–12
½ lb	cooked chicken or pork, cut in bite-sized pieces	250 g
4 tbsp	cashew nuts, toasted	50 mL

1. Set a large pot of water on to boil. Cook the noodles according to the package instructions.
2. In a large mixing bowl, combine all the remaining ingredients except the meat and nuts and whisk to blend together well.
3. When noodles are cooked and drained, add them along with the chicken or pork and cashew nuts to the mixing bowl. Toss gently to coat the noodles well and serve immediately.

THAI CHICKEN WITH HOLY BASIL
AND RED PEPPERS

Serves 4

A specialty of Northern Thailand, this dish combines the mellowness of chicken with the lively properties of fresh "holy" basil with the sweetness of red peppers and the zing of chiles. The botanical name for Thailand's holy basil is *ocimum basilicum* and it is strongly related to the basil more common in North America, except for the blunt shape of its leaves, a more intense basil taste and a slight anise fragrance. Either can be used here. Remember to wear rubber gloves and avoid touching your face when handling fresh chiles.

2 oz	basil leaves	50 g
4 tbsp	vegetable oil	50 mL
1 lb	boneless, skinless chicken breast, finely chopped	500 g
1	red bell pepper, seeded and roughly chopped	1
4	shallots, thinly sliced	4
3 cloves	garlic, chopped	3 cloves
3	red Thai chiles, seeded and finely sliced	3
2 tsp	fresh chopped gingerroot	10 mL
3 tbsp	Thai fish sauce	45 mL
2 tbsp	dark brown sugar	25 mL
	salt	

1. Reserve 6 basil leaves for garnish, and chop the remaining leaves roughly. Place a large skillet or wok over high heat and heat half the oil. Add the chicken and quickly cook it for 2 minutes, stirring so it browns on all sides.
2. Add the red pepper and continue to stir-fry for another minute or so, tossing the meat and pepper so they cook evenly. Transfer the contents of the skillet to a warm bowl and set to one side.
3. Add the remaining oil to the skillet. When it is hot, add the shallots and stir-fry them for no more than a minute; add garlic, chiles and gingerroot and continue to stir-fry for another minute. Add the basil and continue to cook for another minute.

4. Return the chicken and peppers to the skillet and add any accumulated juices, along with the fish sauce and sugar, and stir-fry until everything is just heated through. Transfer to a warm serving platter and garnish with basil. Serve with steamed rice.

LAMB CURRY WITH APRICOTS

Serves 4 to 6

This dish definitely benefits from being prepared a day in advance. If you are able to do this, reheat it gently with an additional splash of water. Instead of *ghee,* you can use 2 tbsp (25 mL) butter combined with 2 tbsp (25 mL) olive oil.

¼ cup	*ghee* (clarified butter)	50 mL
2	medium-sized onions, chopped	2
2 cloves	garlic, finely chopped	2 cloves
1-½ lbs	boneless lamb, cut into 2-inch (5-cm) cubes	680 g
1 cup	plain yogurt	250 mL
1 cup	dried apricots, chopped	250 mL
1 tsp	ginger	5 mL
2 tsp	coriander	10 mL
¼ tsp	cinnamon	1 mL
½ tsp	cardamom	2 mL
¼ tsp	cloves	1 mL
	juice of 1 lemon	
½ cup	water	125 mL

1. In a heavy-based saucepan or Dutch oven, melt the *ghee.* Add onions and garlic and sauté until onion is tender and pale golden, about 5 to 7 minutes. Using a slotted spoon, transfer the onions and garlic to a bowl and reserve.
2. If necessary, add a little more *ghee.* Brown the lamb (in batches) on all sides. Return the onion mixture to the pan. Stir to combine well. Add yogurt and all the remaining ingredients, and stir to combine well. Bring to the boil and reduce heat.
3. Simmer until meat is tender, about 45 minutes. If sauce thickens too much, add a little more water during the cooking time. Serve with basmati rice tossed with a few toasted cashews and a little freshly chopped coriander.

MUM'S LEMON LOAF CAKE WITH WARMED MARMALADE AND CRÈME FRAÎCHE

Makes one 8- x 4-inch (20- x 10-cm) cake

My mum made this wonderful lemony cake regularly and neither I, her grand-daughters nor anyone who ever tasted it grew tired of it. I don't think she would mind my addition of the marmalade sauce and crème fraîche. To warm the marmalade, use your microwave, or set in a small saucepan over medium heat. Stir until a sauce-like consistency is reached; pour it over slices. Try this cake with a glass of Samos or other sweet Greek Muscat.

2	eggs	2
½ cup	milk	125 mL
½ tsp	pure vanilla extract	2 mL
1-½ cups	all-purpose flour	375 mL
1 tsp	baking powder	5 mL
1 cup	sugar	250 mL
	pinch salt	
	juice and finely grated zest of 1 lemon	
½ cup	butter	125 mL
	warmed lemon or orange marmalade, for garnish	
	crème fraîche for garnish	

For the glaze

¼ cup	fresh lemon juice	50 mL
6 tbsp	sugar	90 mL

1. Preheat oven to 350°F (180°C). In a mixing bowl, whisk together the eggs with the milk and vanilla extract. Set aside.

2. In another mixing bowl, combine the flour, baking powder, sugar, salt and lemon zest. Blend well.

3. Using an electric mixer, blend half of the egg mixture with the flour mixture along with the juice of 1 lemon and the butter. Beat on low until dry ingredients are moistened. Gradually add the remaining egg mixture until it is well incorporated and the batter is smooth.

4. Lightly butter the loaf pan and dust it with flour. Scrape batter into the pan and spread it to distribute it evenly. Give the pan one good rap on the counter and place in the preheated oven. Bake for about 55 to 60 minutes or until a cake tester inserted in the centre comes out clean.

5. Meanwhile, make the glaze: in a small saucepan, combine the lemon juice and the sugar. Place the mixture over medium heat and stir continuously until sugar is completely dissolved. Set aside.

6. Remove the cake from the oven and set on a rack. Use a wooden skewer or other thin instrument to make tiny holes in the surface of the cake. Drizzle half the lemon syrup over the surface of the cake. Let cool for 10 minutes in the pan.

7. Carefully turn the cake out onto a rack and repeat Step 6 with the bottom of the cake and some of the lemon syrup. Brush the rest of the syrup onto the sides of the cake. Leave to cool thoroughly and for the glaze to set. Serve in thick slices while warm, with warmed marmalade and crème fraîche.

CHAPTER 5
PINOT BLANC

Pinot Blanc lives under the shadow of its more glamourous sister Chardonnay, for whom it can be mistaken at a glance. (If the truth be known, Pinot Blanc is not related to Chardonnay even though it can confusingly be called Pinot Chardonnay.) What it lacks in popularity it makes up for as a useful and generally less costly variety. A wine to drink young and fresh, it does not have staying power even at its best in Alsace and California. With its high acidity, Pinot Blanc is a good variety for the production of sparkling wines, especially in Alsace.

TASTE PROFILE
Dry, fruity wine with good acidity, usually exhibiting white peach and apple flavours with a high level of alcohol, giving the wine a full mouth feel. Not as complex as Chardonnay but can resemble it with oak treatment.

SYNONYMS
Pinot Bianco (Italy), Weissburgunder (Germany), Clevner (Alsace)

BEST EXPRESSION
Alsace—still and sparkling Crémant d'Alsace; some Northern Italian producers (Tiefenbrunner, Jermann, Cà del Bosco); some Californian and Oregon producers (Chalone, Au Bon Climat, Cameron); Ontario (Konzelmann); British Columbia (Blue Mountain)

SWEET

Austrian late harvest

SUBSTITUTES

Chardonnay, Gavi, Soave

THE WINE LOVER COOKS

KEDGEREE

Kedgeree—or *kitcherie*—is an old Anglo-Indian dish and a typical example of cooking from the time of the British Raj in India. Its name originates from the Hindi *khichri,* which describes a pan of rice cooked with butter and lentils with the addition of spices and perhaps fried onions. The kedgeree enjoyed by the British in India (like the recipe that follows) invariably included fresh or smoked haddock or kippers, chunks of hard-boiled egg and rice, with a little turmeric and cayenne for colour and flavour.

½ lb	smoked haddock	250 g
½ cup	milk	125 mL
4 tbsp	unsalted butter	50 mL
	pinch freshly grated nutmeg	
1 tsp	turmeric	5 mL
½ tsp	cayenne	2 mL
½ tsp	salt	2 mL
¼ tsp	white pepper	1 mL
2-½ cups	cooked, long-grain rice	625 mL
1 tbsp	white wine vinegar	15 mL
2	hard-boiled eggs, chopped	2
3 tbsp	chopped fresh parsley	45 mL

1. In a shallow pan, bring milk with ½ cup (125 mL) of water to a gentle boil. Gently poach the haddock until fish flakes easily with a fork, about 12 minutes. Drain and, when cool enough to handle, remove and discard any bones or skin. Flake the fish into a bowl and set aside.

2. In a medium-sized skillet, melt the butter over medium-high heat. Add the nutmeg, turmeric, cayenne, salt and white pepper, and cook gently for a minute or so to enable spices to lose their raw taste. Add cooked rice and vinegar, and cook for 5 to 6 minutes until rice is well heated and blended with the spice mixture.

3. Add the reserved fish and chopped eggs and stir to combine well. Cook until everything is piping hot, sprinkle with chopped parsley and serve immediately, garnished with thickly sliced ripe tomatoes and hot buttered toast.

RISOTTO WITH BUTTERNUT SQUASH

Serves 4 to 6

A lovely risotto for fall, this makes the perfect prelude to roast pork or chicken.

5–6 cups	homemade (or good quality) chicken broth	1.25–1.5 L
2 tbsp	butter	25 mL
4 tbsp	extra virgin olive oil	50 mL
1	onion, finely chopped	1
2 cloves	garlic, minced	2 cloves
1	medium-sized acorn or butternut squash, peeled, seeded, finely chopped	1
2 cups	short-grained Italian arborio rice	500 mL
½ cup	dry white wine	125 mL
1 cup	grated Parmigiano Reggiano	250 mL
1 tbsp	finely chopped oregano	15 mL
1 tbsp	finely chopped flat-leaf parsley	15 mL

1. In a large saucepan, bring the broth to a boil over high heat. Reduce heat to achieve a slow simmer and keep the broth at this steady, slightly bubbling level throughout the rest of the cooking.

2. In a heavy-based, deep casserole or skillet, heat the butter and the oil over medium-high heat. Add the onion and sauté just until it becomes translucent, about 2 minutes; add garlic, sauté for another 2 minutes and then add the squash, stirring to combine well. Add rice, all at once. Pour in wine, and cook, stirring for 1 minute or until wine is evaporated.

3. Stir and sauté rice until all the grains are well coated and glistening with the butter and oil mixture; this will take about 2 minutes.

4. Use a ladle to add hot broth, ½ cup (125 mL) at a time, to the pan. If you find the broth evaporates too quickly, reduce heat a little. Stir the rice constantly to keep it from sticking. Don't add more broth until you can see the rice drying out and the liquid disappearing.

5. Repeat, ladling in the hot broth a bit at a time and stir-cooking, scraping the bottom and sides of the pan, for about 15 minutes. As you near the end of the cooking time, add broth only about 1/4 cup (50 mL) at a time—you may not need every bit of it.

6. Cook until rice is tender but with a firm heart and overall creaminess; it should not be soupy or runny looking. Just before serving, add the cheese, oregano and parsley, and combine well. You may not need to add salt but add a few twists of the pepper mill. Serve immediately.

FRENCH ONION TART

Serves 6

Any type of onion may be used in this recipe. Just make sure to allow enough cooking time for the onions to caramelize and darken. Serve with grilled sausages and a bitter green salad.

4 tbsp	butter	50 mL
1 lb	onions, very thinly sliced	500 g
½ tsp	salt	2 mL
¼ tsp	freshly ground black pepper	1 mL
3	eggs	3
½ cup	milk	125 mL
½ cup	light cream	125 mL
¼ tsp	freshly grated nutmeg	1 mL
1	10-in (25-cm) baked pastry shell	1

1. In a large skillet, melt butter over medium heat. Add onions, salt and pepper; stir to combine. Cover and cook, stirring occasionally, until onions begin to caramelize, about 30 minutes. Remove from heat and set to one side. Preheat oven to 350°F (180°C).
2. In a mixing bowl, combine the eggs with the milk, cream and nutmeg. Whisk together until well blended. Spread cooled onions over the surface of the baked pastry shell. Pour the egg mixture over the onions. Bake in preheated oven until filling is set, about 30 minutes. Serve warm.

HUEVOS RANCHEROS

Serves 6

Any Mexican dish that features *ranchero* or *a la ranchera* in its name refers to the rough, *picante* tomato sauce in which the dish is cooked. The heat could come from *serranos* (also known as *habaneros* or Scotch bonnet peppers), dried chiles like chipotles (smoked jalapeños), or any one of a number of other chiles. This version of the classic Mexican brunch dish is slightly more contemporary than the original, but a little easier to put together.

3 tbsp	olive oil	45 mL
2	large onions, chopped	2
1	medium-sized green bell pepper, chopped	1
2 cloves	garlic, minced	2 cloves
4 cups	canned plum tomatoes, drained, chopped	1 L
2–3	jalapeños, finely chopped (or to taste)	2–3
½ tsp	dried Mexican oregano (or regular oregano)	2 mL
½ tsp	cumin	2 mL
¼ tsp	salt	1 mL
¼ tsp	freshly ground black pepper	1 mL
6–8	eggs	6–8
6	corn tortillas, warmed	6
½ cup	crumbled *queso fresco* (fresh cheese), or a mild feta or farmer's cheese	125 mL
¼ cup	chopped fresh parsley	50 mL

1. In a large, wide skillet, heat the oil over medium-high heat. Sauté the onions, green pepper and garlic until softened, about 5 minutes.

2. Add tomatoes, jalapeños, oregano, cumin, salt and pepper; stir to combine well and cook at a brisk simmer for 10 minutes or so, until sauce thickens and flavours are well blended. Cover and reduce heat to low.

3. Break the eggs into a large, nonstick skillet set over medium heat. Sprinkle with a little salt and pepper and cook slowly until they are done to your preference. To set the tops of the eggs, add a little warm water to the pan and cover with a lid. Check after 10 or 15 seconds, at which time the resulting steam should have helped to cook the tops of the eggs.

4. To assemble the dish, place a warmed tortilla on each of six plates, top with one or two fried eggs, then spoon the sauce over the tortilla and whites of the eggs, leaving the yolks exposed. Sprinkle with the cheese and a little chopped parsley and serve immediately.

FRITTATA WITH SWISS CHARD AND PANCETTA

Serves 4 to 6

Nice for a light evening meal or as part of an antipasti selection, the Italian omelette known as frittata lends itself to a myriad of additions. This is a particularly nice version studded with brilliant Swiss chard and unsmoked bacon.

1 lb	Swiss chard, washed, stemmed, chopped	500 g
3 tbsp	olive oil	45 mL
¼ lb	pancetta	125 g
1	onion, finely chopped	1
	salt and freshly ground black pepper	
8	eggs	8
3 tbsp	fresh breadcrumbs	45 mL
3 tbsp	grated pecorino romano cheese	45 mL
2 tsp	light cream	10 mL

1. Rinse the Swiss chard and place in a large skillet; cook it with no additional liquid. Drain and squeeze dry; set it aside. Add oil to the same skillet and sauté the pancetta and onion for 6 minutes, until bacon is cooked and onion softened. Add the Swiss chard, salt and pepper, and continue to cook for another 5 minutes or so, stirring to combine all ingredients.

2. Preheat broiler. In a mixing bowl, whisk the eggs with the breadcrumbs, cheese and cream until well blended. Add this mixture to the skillet, gently running a narrow metal spatula around the edges of the pan to lift the cooked egg up and allow any uncooked egg mixture to run beneath; cook for 5 minutes or so until frittata is set and cooked on the bottom.

3. Place skillet 6 inches (15 cm) beneath broiler. Cook 2 minutes or until top is set and golden brown. Serve immediately or cooled to room temperature, cut into squares or strips.

SPANISH BOUILLABAISSE

Serves 4 to 6

A magnificently flavourful dish, this fish stew with a Spanish flair is easy to put together. Before serving, toast or grill thick slices of bread, rub them with a cut garlic clove and drizzle with Spanish olive oil. Serve the bread alongside the bouillabaisse. Don't omit the ground almond and garlic mixture; that is what makes this recipe thoroughly Spanish. If you like, ask your fishmonger to trim, slice and bone the fish, but make sure the trimmings are included.

4 cups	water	1 L
3-½ lbs	red snapper, trimmed and sliced into 2-inch (5-cm) pieces	1.75 kg
¼ cup	olive oil	50 mL
2 tbsp	unsalted butter	25 mL
2	onions, finely chopped	2
2	large, ripe tomatoes, skinned, seeded and chopped	2
2 tbsp	chopped fresh parsley	25 mL
1	bay leaf	1
1 tsp	dried thyme	5 mL
2 cups	Pinot Blanc	500 mL
	salt and freshly ground black pepper	
20	blanched, toasted almonds	20
2 cloves	garlic	2 cloves
	chopped fresh parsley for garnish	

1. In a large saucepan, bring the water to a boil. Lightly salt it and add the fish bones and trimmings. Gently boil for about half an hour, strain and reserve a little more than 2 cups (500 mL) of the fish stock.

2. In a Dutch oven or similar pot, heat the oil and butter over medium heat. Add onions and cook until softened, about 6 minutes. Add tomatoes and simmer for another 5 minutes.

3. Add fish stock, parsley, bay leaf, and thyme, and bring to a boil. Add wine, salt, pepper, and simmer for about 15 minutes.

4. Chop the toasted almonds together with the garlic. Transfer the mixture to a pestle and mortar and, along with a pinch of salt, grind the nuts and garlic until a smooth paste forms. (This can also be done in a blender or small electric chopper.) Add this paste to the hot fish stock as it simmers, stirring to blend well.

5. Carefully place the sliced red snapper pieces in the liquid, making sure they are submerged. Bring the liquid back to a gentle boil, reduce heat immediately and simmer until fish is cooked through, about 20 minutes. Pour into a heated soup tureen and serve at the table, ladled over toasted bread in soup plates and sprinkled with chopped parsley.

COLD CHICKEN BREASTS WITH
TOMATO BASIL VINAIGRETTE

Serves 4 to 6

Here is a delightful summer dish that is substantial enough to serve as a light main course. The tomato and basil vinaigrette is also terrific with grilled fish steaks, pasta or greens. To make things even easier, poach the chicken breasts the day before; cool it, cover with plastic wrap and refrigerate overnight. Allow the chicken to return to room temperature before serving with the vinaigrette.

5	large boneless, chicken breasts, slightly flattened to a uniform thickness	5
1	small lemon, thinly sliced	1
1	bouquet garni (bay leaf, parsley, fresh thyme, celery top or length of leek tied together)	1
1	large onion, sliced	1
1	carrot, sliced	1
8	peppercorns	8
4 cups	chicken broth	1 L
1 cup	Pinot Blanc	250 mL

For the vinaigrette

1 bunch	fresh basil, stems removed	1 bunch
2 cloves	garlic, roughly chopped	2 cloves
2 tbsp	fresh lemon juice	25 mL
⅓ cup	extra virgin olive oil	75 mL
	salt and freshly ground black pepper	
	pinch sugar	
1 lb	fresh ripe tomatoes, skinned, seeded and finely diced	500 g
3 tbsp	capers, drained	45 mL

THE WINE LOVER COOKS

1. Place the chicken breasts in a large, deep skillet or Dutch oven. Add lemon slices, bouquet garni, onion, carrot and peppercorns, and cover with chicken broth and wine. Bring to a gentle boil; then immediately reduce heat to a simmer, cover and cook very gently for 25 minutes, until chicken is cooked. (Don't allow liquid to boil, as the chicken will become tough.)

2. Use tongs to remove chicken from poaching liquid and let cool. Discard the liquid. When it is cool enough to handle, remove and discard the skin, and slice the breasts on an angle into relatively thick slices. Set aside while preparing the vinaigrette.

3. To make the vinaigrette, place the basil, garlic, lemon juice and oil in a blender or food processor. Process until smooth. Scrape mixture into a bowl and add salt, pepper and sugar and blend well. Add diced tomatoes and, if necessary, add a little more oil or lemon to balance flavours.

4. To serve, pour most of the vinaigrette onto a large platter. Arrange chicken in overlapping slices on top. Drizzle with the remaining vinaigrette and sprinkle with capers. Serve immediately with thin slices of warmed baguette.

COD PROVENÇAL

Serves 6 to 8

Filled with the flavours of sunny Provence—and featuring that area's famed ingredients—this makes a lovely summer dish, and tastes just as good at room temperature as it does hot. Make sure to use thinly cut fish fillets or steaks. Serve a simple rice salad alongside, with lots of warm, crusty bread.

¼ cup	extra virgin olive oil	50 mL
1	large onion, very thinly sliced	1
2 cloves	garlic, finely chopped	2 cloves
1	red bell pepper, seeded and shredded	1
1	small can (2 oz/50mL) anchovies, rinsed, dried, chopped	1
½ cup	pitted black olives	125 mL
¼ tsp	fennel seeds	1 mL
8	cod fillets or steaks, ½ inch (1 cm) thick	8
1–2	large ripe tomatoes, thickly sliced	1–2
	salt and freshly ground black pepper	
½ cup	tomato paste	125 mL
1 cup	Pinot Blanc	250 mL
¼ cup	chopped fresh parsley	50 mL

1. Preheat oven to 400°F (200°C). In a large skillet, heat half the oil over medium-high heat. Add onion, garlic and red pepper, and cook for 6 to 7 minutes, until softened. Add anchovies, olives and fennel, stir to combine well and cook for another minute or so.

2. In a greased glass baking dish, lay four of the pieces of fish in a single layer and cover with anchovy mixture. Top each piece with the remaining pieces of fish and then add a slice of tomato. Drizzle with the remaining olive oil and season to taste.

3. Blend the tomato paste with the wine and pour over the fish. Bake for no more than 30 minutes, basting with the liquid from time to time. Just before serving, sprinkle with chopped parsley.

CHAPTER 6

PINOT GRIS/ PINOT GRIGIO

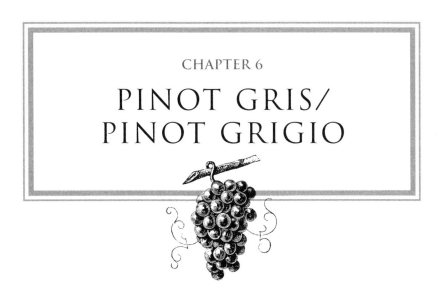

The grey Pinot is a mutation of Pinot Noir, the grape that produces red Burgundy. Pinot Gris has a skin colour that can vary from blue to brownish pink, and this chameleon character carries over to the wine produced from it. Depending on the soil conditions and climate, it can produce a light, spritzy, pale wine in Northern Italy, when picked slightly underripe, to a rich, unctuous, honeyed, deeply coloured wine in Alsace capable of late harvesting.

TASTE PROFILE

Usually rich and peachy-melon with a hint of spice and low acidity. In cooler climates it tends to be more acidic. When attacked by botrytis (noble rot), it produces deep golden wines with concentrated honeyed flavours.

SYNONYMS

Tokay d'Alsace, Pinot Grigio (Italy), Grauburgunder (Germany, dry), Ruländer (Germany, sweet), Szürkebarat (Hungary)

BEST EXPRESSIONS

Alsace Pinot Gris, Oregon Pinot Gris

DRIEST

Pinot Grigio from Northern Italy

SWEET

Vendange Tardive and Sélection de Grains Nobles (Alsace), Grauburgunder or Ruländer Auslese and higher sugar levels

SUBSTITUTES

warm-climate Chardonnay, Sémillon

CREAM OF WILD MUSHROOM SOUP

Serves 6

This is, quite simply, the most magnificent cream soup you'll ever make. It sends mushroom lovers straight to heaven with a swoon. Any combination of mushrooms can be used, but make sure to use some domestic along with chanterelles, shiitake and portobello, and include some rehydrated porcini. Add the water that the dried mushrooms soaked in, being careful to strain it through a cloth-lined sieve, into the chicken stock.

1 lb	assorted mushrooms (button, chanterelles, shiitake, portobello, trumpet)	500 g
2–4 oz	dried porcini, rehydrated	60–125 g
3 tbsp	unsalted butter	45 mL
2 cloves	garlic, finely chopped	2 cloves
3	medium-sized shallots, chopped	3
2 tsp	herbes de Provence	10 mL
	salt and freshly ground pepper	
2-½ cups	chicken broth	625 mL
3 cups	heavy cream	750 mL

1. Wipe the fresh mushrooms clean. Coarsely chop them, along with the rehydrated mushrooms, either by hand or in a food processor.
2. In a heavy saucepan or soup pot, melt the butter over medium-high heat. Sauté the garlic and shallots with the herbes de Provence, until the garlic and shallots are softened, about 5 minutes. Add mushrooms and continue to sauté for about 10 minutes, stirring occasionally.
3. Add salt, pepper and chicken broth, bring to a gentle boil and then reduce heat, add cream and allow mixture to simmer gently for 20 minutes. Serve immediately.

PESTO CREPES WITH GRILLED SWORDFISH

Makes 12 to 16 appetizers

If you don't want to fire up the grill for just two fish steaks, pan-fry or roast the steaks instead. Or, if you plan on using the grill for dinner the day before, grill the swordfish ahead of time, cool it, wrap it in plastic and refrigerate it until you're ready to put the recipe together. Allow the fish to come to room temperature before using it, or reheat it gently in the microwave. Use a store-bought pesto sauce to speed things up, unless you have a good supply of home-grown basil!

If you cannot find crème fraîche, it is very easy to make your own: Combine 1 cup (250 mL) heavy cream with 2 tbsp (25 mL) buttermilk in a glass container. Cover and let stand at room temperature overnight or until it becomes very thick. Stir well before covering and refrigerating for up to 10 days.

For the crepes

½ cup	milk	125 mL
1 cup	all-purpose flour	250 mL
1-½ tsp	baking powder	7 mL
⅛ tsp	salt	½ mL
1	egg	1
2 tbsp	pesto	25 mL
	vegetable oil, as needed for frying	
1 cup	crème fraîche	250 mL
2	boneless swordfish or tuna steaks (4oz/ 120 g each) ½-inch (1-cm) thick, grilled and cut into chunks	2
¼ cup	pine nuts, toasted	50 mL
	salt and freshly ground black pepper	
12–16	fresh basil leaves for garnish	12–16

1. Pour half of the milk into a mixing bowl. Add the flour, baking powder, salt, egg and pesto, and, using a wire whisk or fork, mix to a smooth batter. Add the remainder of the milk and stir until the batter is well blended.

2. In a large nonstick frying pan, warm just enough oil to cover the surface. Swirl it around the pan, then spoon large spoonfuls of the crepe batter into the pan, just enough to make individual-sized crepes.

3. Wait about 30 seconds, then flip the crepe to cook on the other side for about the same length of time. Keep crepes warm as you remove them from the pan. Continue this procedure until all the batter has been used.

4. To serve, arrange the crepes on a serving platter; top each one with a bit of crème fraîche, a chunk of grilled fish, a sprinkling of pine nuts, salt and a grind or two of pepper, and a few leaves of basil.

MUSSEL SOUP WITH CREAM AND GARLIC

Serves 4

A classic first course in the best French bistro tradition, this very rich soup should be accompanied by lots of warm, crusty bread. With a lively mixed green salad as a precursor and a well-balanced cheese course to follow, this substantial soup also easily makes a lovely main course.

2 lbs	mussels, cleaned, debearded	1 kg
3 cloves	garlic, roughly chopped	3 cloves
2	shallots, chopped	2
2	small white onions, quartered	2
2 large sprigs	parsley	2 large sprigs
	salt and freshly ground black pepper	
	pinch cayenne	
1 cup	Pinot Gris	250 mL
2 tbsp	butter	25 mL
1 tsp	herbes de Provence	5 mL
2 cups	heavy cream	500 mL
¼ cup	chopped fresh parsley	50 mL

1. In a large, deep saucepan or Dutch oven, combine the mussels with the garlic, shallots, onions, parsley, salt, pepper, cayenne, wine, butter and herbes de Provence. Cover and bring to a gentle boil. Reduce heat and simmer until most of the mussels have opened. Remove from heat and discard any unopened mussels.

2. Pour the contents of the pan into a cheesecloth-lined sieve set over a bowl and allow to drain for a few minutes. Remove the mussels from their shells, discarding shells. Wipe the saucepan clean and return the cooking liquid to it.

3. Bring the liquid to a boil and slowly add cream. Let it return to a gentle boil, reduce heat and simmer for a few minutes until slightly thickened; then remove from heat. (If mixture seems too thin, add a beaten egg yolk and return the pan to the heat long enough to thicken.)

4. Add mussels to the saucepan, stir thoroughly, and cover for 5 minutes. Serve garnished with fresh parsley and plenty of crusty bread.

GRILLED VEAL CHOPS WITH PEACH SALSA

Serves 6

Succulent veal chops need little in the way of embellishment. However, the fresh fruit salsa in this recipe provides just the right refreshing accent to complement the meat's delicate flavour.

For the salsa

2	ripe peaches, peeled, chopped	2
½ cup	prepared salsa (not overly spicy)	125 mL
1	small red onion, minced	1
2 tbsp	lemon or lime juice	25 mL
2 tbsp	chopped fresh parsley	25 mL

For the chops

½ tsp	lemon or lime zest, minced	2 mL
6	veal rib or loin chops, cut ¾–1-inch (2–2.5-cm) thick	6
4 tbsp	olive oil	50 mL
	salt and freshly ground black pepper	

1. In medium bowl, combine the peaches, prepared salsa, onion, lemon or lime juice and parsley. Blend well, cover and refrigerate until it is time to serve the chops.

2. Rub lemon or lime zest well into chops. Drizzle with oil (both sides) and add a little salt and pepper. Grill chops over medium-hot heat 12 to 14 minutes or to desired doneness, turning once or twice. Serve with peach salsa.

SAGE AND GARLIC PORK WITH APRICOT CHUTNEY

Serves 8 to 10

Make the chutney accompaniment for this dish ahead of time. Team this fragrant roast with a New World Pinot Gris. This recipe works equally well with a lean roast of veal.

For the apricot chutney

1 tbsp	vegetable oil	15 mL
2	medium onions, sliced	2
6 oz	dried apricots, coarsely chopped	185 g
1 cup	chicken broth	250 mL
1-½ tsp	cider vinegar	7 mL
½ tsp	dried thyme	2 mL

For the roast

1 tsp	dry sage	5 mL
2 cloves	garlic, minced	2 cloves
½ tsp	coarsely ground black pepper	2 mL
1 tbsp	vegetable oil	15 mL
3 lbs	boneless pork roast	1.5 kg

1. In a skillet over medium heat, heat the oil and sauté the onions until soft, stirring occasionally, about 5 minutes. Stir in the apricots, chicken broth, vinegar and thyme, and mix to combine all the ingredients. Bring to a gentle boil, then reduce heat to allow mixture to simmer for about 20 to 25 minutes or until apricots are soft, stirring occasionally. When mixture has thickened, remove it from the heat and set it aside.

2. Preheat oven to 325°F (160°C). In a small bowl, combine the sage, garlic, pepper and oil. Rub this mixture into the surface of the meat. Place meat, fat side up, on rack in roasting pan. Roast in preheated oven for approximately 25 minutes per pound (500 g) for medium doneness.

3. Remove roast from oven and let stand 15 minutes before carving. Carve into thick slices and serve with apricot chutney.

CHAPTER 7

RIESLING

As a grape variety, Riesling makes some of the best bone-dry wines on this planet and some of the finest dessert wines—and every shade of sweetness in between. With its fine spine of acidity and spicy complexity, it is the most versatile of wines for matching with cuisines as diverse as French, Mexican, Thai and Californian. It even goes well with light curries.

No dry white wine ages as long or as beautifully as Riesling, with the possible exception of Chenin Blanc from the Loire. A Schloss Schönborn Johannisberger Vintage 1735 from the Reingau was opened a few years ago and found to be still alive and drinking well. Not that I'm advocating you leave your Riesling to mature for 250 years, but don't be despondent if you neglect it in your cellar for a decade or two.

A chef in the Vosges Mountains once told me that the dry Riesling of his native Alsace was like "a naked sword." The simile was apt. At its best, Riesling from cool regions has a brightness in the glass, a racy crispness and a mouth-freshening brilliance of citrus and floral flavours unlike any other wine. It is clean and long and shining, just like a sword. Naked, because it is unadorned. What you get from the vineyard is what you work with in the cellar. You can't improve a Riesling by fancy vinting techniques or disguising its flaws with overpowering oak flavours.

Riesling is uncompromising: what's in the grape is what you get. Put another way, Riesling is a sculpture chiselled from a block of stone; Chardonnay is a sculpture you build up by adding clay to clay. There is no room for error in Riesling; Chardonnay you can fudge.

TASTE PROFILE

In cool climates such as Germany, Austria, Alsace, Ontario and New York State, Riesling has a racy acidity ameliorated by the amount of sugar in the grapes at the time of harvest or by the amount of residual sugar left in the wine after fermentation (this is accomplished either by stopping the fermentation before the wine has been fermented to dryness or by adding sweet reserve to the finished wine).

Riesling is a highly aromatic wine; it offers floral notes with citrus flavours. As it gets riper, it exhibits peach and apricot flavours with a lemony-grapefruit finish. As it ages, it takes on a characteristic petrol or kerosene quality on the nose.

SYNONYMS

White (Weisser) Riesling, Johannisberg Riesling, Rhine Riesling, Riesling Renano (Italy).

BEST EXPRESSION

light bodied—Mosel and Reingau; medium-bodied—Rheinhessen, Pfalz; fuller-bodied—Alsace, Austria, New York, Ontario.

German and Austrian label designations tell you the sweetness of the wine:

QbA: the driest

Kabinett: dry but fruity

Spätlese (late-harvest): medium sweet

Auslese (selectively picked late harvest): honeyed sweet

Beerenauslese/Eiswein: sweet and rich

Trockenbeerenauslese: unctuously sweet

(Austria has a unique designation of sweetness between Beeren and Trockenbeerenauslese styles, namely Ausbruch, wines made from totally botrytized, or "nobly rotten," grapes.)

A further wrinkle: Within each category of sugar level from QbA to Auslese, Germany has three styles of wine: Trocken (dry), Halbtrocken (medium-dry) and Lieblich (sweet). Riesling QbA Trocken and Kabinett Trocken are two of the driest wines you can find.

SUBSTITUTES

dry Muscat

FIVE-SPICE ORANGE PORK TENDERLOIN

Serves 6

Look for five-spice powder in Asian supermarkets and many regular super-markets. Or make your own by blending equal amounts of cinnamon, cloves, fennel seed, star anise and Szechwan (or regular) peppercorns.

3	whole pork tenderloins, about 2 lb (1 kg) total	3
	salt and freshly ground black pepper	
	all-purpose flour for dredging	
2 tbsp	butter	25 mL
1 cup	chicken broth	250 mL
½ cup	fresh orange juice, with pulp	125 mL
2 tsp	five-spice powder	10 mL
1 tbsp	grated orange zest	15 mL

1. Preheat oven to lowest setting. Cut the pork into medallions and flatten them slightly with a kitchen mallet or rolling pin. Season with salt and pepper and then dredge in the flour, shaking off any excess.

2. Heat butter in a heavy skillet over medium-high heat and brown the meat for 1 minute on each side, turning only once. Place pork on a platter and keep warm in the oven.

3. Add chicken broth and orange juice to the pan, and bring to a boil over medium heat, stirring to dissolve any brown bits in the pan. Add five-spice powder and orange zest, and increase the heat to high. Boil the sauce, stirring, until it coats the back of a spoon, about 6 to 8 minutes.

4. Return medallions to the pan and cook in the sauce for a minute or two, turning once to coat meat.

5. Arrange on serving plates and divide sauce over each serving. Serve with rice and green beans tossed with slivered, toasted almonds.

GRILLED CITRUS TUNA

Serves 6

When citrus is paired with fresh fish in a marinade, it is important not to let the fish marinate longer than necessary, as the acid in the citrus will begin to "cook" it. If the price of tuna is prohibitive, swordfish makes a good substitute. A New World Riesling is a good choice for this dish.

½ cup	light soy sauce	125 mL
½ cup	fresh orange juice	125 mL
3 tbsp	hoisin sauce	45 mL
1 tbsp	tomato paste	15 mL
¼ cup	chopped fresh parsley	50 mL
2 tbsp	fresh lemon juice	25 mL
1 tsp	freshly ground black pepper	5 mL
2 cloves	garlic, minced	2 cloves
6	tuna steaks, 1-inch/2.5-cm thick (about 2 lbs/1 kg)	6

1. In a shallow dish large enough to accommodate the fish in one layer, combine the soy sauce, orange juice, hoisin sauce, tomato paste, parsley, lemon juice, pepper and garlic. Combine well.
2. Add tuna, cover with plastic wrap and refrigerate for half an hour.
3. Preheat grill to high. Remove fish from refrigerator and allow to return to room temperature. Grill fish for about 5 to 6 minutes on each side or to desired doneness, using the marinade as a basting sauce. Serve immediately.

SAMBAL GORENG

Serves 6

Spiced chicken livers with lots of garlic and green beans is a popular Indonesian dish. All it needs as an accompaniment is lots of simply cooked rice and perhaps a lightly dressed fresh cucumber and cherry tomato salad. Reduce the amount of garlic if it is too excessive for your taste.

3 tbsp	peanut oil	45 mL
1 lb	chicken livers, trimmed, halved	500 g
8–10 cloves	garlic, minced	8–10 cloves
1 tsp	minced fresh gingerroot	5 mL
3	small shallots, minced	3
1 lb	thin green beans, trimmed and cut in ½-inch/1-cm pieces	500 g
2 tbsp	fresh lemon juice	25 mL
1 tbsp	*ketjap manis* (Indonesian soy sauce)	15 mL
1 cup	chicken broth	250 mL
1 tsp	salt	5 mL
1 tsp	cayenne	5 mL
2 tsp	brown sugar	10 mL
2 tsp	turmeric	10 mL

1. In a large skillet, heat the oil over high heat and stir-fry the chicken livers until lightly browned. Transfer them to a bowl and set aside.
2. Reduce heat to medium and add the garlic, ginger and shallots to the skillet. Cook for about 5 minutes until softened. Add green beans and cook for another 2 to 3 minutes.
3. Add lemon juice, soy sauce, chicken broth, salt, cayenne, brown sugar and turmeric; stir to blend all the ingredients and cook for another 10 minutes, until beans are tender.
4. Return the chicken livers to the skillet and cook for another 5 minutes. Serve immediately.

SMOKED TURKEY TOSTADAS WITH SALSA CRUDA

Serves 6 to 8

The *salsa cruda* in this light and colourful appetizer is made of small amounts of chopped onion, jalapeños, ripe tomatoes, fresh coriander, and a little salt and pepper. Vary the ingredients to your taste or use a favourite commercially prepared salsa. You can also buy canned black beans instead of preparing the dried variety. Choose small corn tortillas for this dish.

For the smoky black beans

1-½ cups	dried black beans	375 mL
7 cups	water	1.75 L
½ lb	bacon	250 g
1	large onion, diced	1
3 cloves	garlic, minced	3 cloves
2 tsp	cumin	10 mL
2 tsp	coriander	10 mL
1	large ripe tomato, peeled and chopped	1
	salt and freshly ground black pepper	

To assemble the tostadas

	vegetable oil	
12–16	corn tortillas	12–16
	smoky black beans (see above recipe)	
2 cups	shredded lettuce	500 mL
2 cups	shredded smoked turkey breast	500 mL
1-½ cups	crumbled *queso fresco* (Mexican fresh white cheese or farmer's cheese)	625 mL
2 cups	*salsa cruda*	500 mL
1 cup	sour cream	250 mL

To make the smoky black beans:

1. Sort, wash and soak the beans in water to cover overnight, changing the water twice. Drain the beans and place them with the water in a large pot;

bring it to a boil. Immediately reduce the heat to moderate and cook for 1-½ to 2 hours until the beans are very tender.

2. Meanwhile, cook the bacon in a large skillet until crisp. Remove the bacon from the skillet with a slotted spoon and drain it on paper towels. Discard (or save for another use) all but ¼ cup (50 mL) of the fat. When the bacon is cool enough to handle, chop it coarsely and set aside.

3. Add the onion, garlic, cumin and coriander to the bacon fat in the pan and cook over moderate heat for 15 minutes, stirring from time to time. Add tomato and cook 15 minutes.

4. When the beans are done, drain off any excess liquid and combine them with the onion mixture and the bacon; mix well and adjust the seasoning. Set aside and keep hot.

To assemble tostadas:

1. In a large skillet, heat a thin layer of oil over moderately high heat until the oil is hot but not smoking. Add one tortilla and cook until it is crisp around the edges; turn and cook on the other side until the edges are crisp but the tortilla is still soft in the centre. Remove tortilla to drain on paper towels and keep warm.

2. Repeat Step 1 for remaining tortillas. Place tortillas on individual plates. Top with some of the hot beans, a bit of lettuce, turkey, cheese and *salsa cruda.* Serve at room temperature and garnish with sour cream.

CRACKED CRAB AND
HONEYDEW MELON SALAD

Serves 6

"Impressive without fuss" neatly sums up this sweet, fresh-tasting salad, which is everything a summer salad should be—cool, refreshing and delicious. This is also very good combined with cooked pasta.

1 lb	cooked crab (preferably fresh, but frozen or canned will do)	500 g
½ cup	quality mayonnaise	125 mL
3 tbsp	thick, plain yogurt	45 mL
2 tbsp	extra virgin olive oil	25 mL
	juice of 1 large lemon	
3	thin green onions, finely chopped	3
2 tbsp	chopped fresh coriander	25 mL
2 tbsp	chopped fresh mint	25 mL
2 tsp	hot sauce	10 mL
1 large (or 2 small)	honeydew melons, peeled, seeded, thinly sliced	1 large (or 2 small)
2 heads	Boston lettuce, washed, dried, leaves separated	2 heads
	salt and freshly ground black pepper	

1. Pick over the crabmeat, discarding any shell or cartilage. Pull the crabmeat apart carefully into good-sized chunks.

2. In a mixing bowl, combine the mayonnaise, yogurt, olive oil, lemon juice, green onions, coriander, mint and hot sauce. Blend together well with a fork or whisk. Gently fold the crabmeat into the mixture.

3. Divide the slices of melon and lettuce leaves between six serving plates. Nestle the crabmeat mixture in between the melon and lettuce on each plate. Season to taste and serve immediately.

CHAPTER 8
SAUVIGNON BLANC

A white variety extensively grown in Bordeaux, where it is customarily blended with Sémillon, Sauvignon Blanc has achieved more fame and fans either as the tart, refreshing wines of Sancerre and Pouilly-Fumé or as the more generous Sauvignons of New Zealand. In warmer growing regions, it lacks a zingy freshness, especially when fermented or aged in oak. But California Sauvignon, sometimes styled as Fumé Blanc, can take on a richness and exhibit complex fruit aromas and flavours, similar to Chardonnay albeit with an underlying herbaceous character. These dry wines are very versatile when it comes to matching with food because of their driving acidity.

In the Sautérnes and Barsac regions of Bordeaux, Sauvignon achieves another distinction when blended (in small proportion) with Sémillon to create the honey-sweet dessert wines of the region. The grapes for these wines are affected by botrytis (noble rot). California and Chile also produce sweet versions of Sauvignon Blanc.

TASTE PROFILE

Sauvignon Blanc's major flavour components are grassiness and green fruits, particularly gooseberries, elderberries and figs. Other green fruits and vegetables are also detectable—peapods, asparagus, green beans, green peppers. In really ripe Sauvignon, particularly from New Zealand, you'll find nettles, passionfruit, papaya and other tropical fruit flavours, invariably with a firm acid base. There is also a tendency when overcropped to produced aromas of the cat's tray.

SYNONYMS

Sauvignon Jaune, Blanc Fumé, Fumé Blanc

BEST EXPRESSION

dry—Sancerre and the more full-bodied Pouilly-Fumé and the lesser Loire villages of Menetou-Salon, Quincy and Reuilly; New Zealand's Marlborough and Martinborough; riper style—Napa, Sonoma; sweet—Late-Harvest Sauvignon Blanc from California and Chile, Sautérnes and Barsac

SUBSTITUTES

Sémillon, Muscadet, Chenin Blanc

SAVOURY FRITTERS

Makes about 50

I enjoyed these delightful little bread fritters many times while in southern Italy's Apulia region. Sometimes they were studded with either black olives, capers, red pepper or bits of cooked cauliflower, salt cod or anchovies.

1 pkg	active dry yeast (not quick-rise yeast)	1 pkg
½ cup	lukewarm water	125 mL
1-¼–1-½ cups	lukewarm water	300–375 mL
2-½–3 cups	all-purpose flour	625–750 mL
1 tsp	salt	5 mL
½ cup	roughly chopped pitted black olives	125 mL
1	small onion, finely chopped	1
¼ tsp	crushed red pepper flakes (optional)	1 mL
	pure olive oil for frying (or other vegetable oil with a high smoking point)	

1. In a large warmed mixing bowl, combine the yeast in ½ cup (125 mL) of the lukewarm water and allow to sit for about 5 minutes or until foamy and bubbling. Stir to make sure yeast is entirely dissolved. Add another cup of lukewarm water, most of the flour and salt, and mix well. Add more water, if necessary, to achieve a rather wet, sticky, batter-like dough. It shouldn't resemble bread dough.

2. Stir in the black olives, onion and red pepper flakes. Cover with plastic wrap and a tea towel, and place in a warm place for about 1 hour until dough has risen to double its size. Preheat oven to 200°F (93°C). Line a baking sheet with paper towels.

3. In a deep-frying pan, electric deep-fryer or Dutch oven, pour in enough oil to come to a depth of about 3 inches (8 cm). Heat oil over medium-high heat to 350°F (180°C).

4. Drop heaping spoonfuls of the dough-batter into the hot oil, about a dozen at a time (don't crowd). Fry the dough balls, until golden brown, turning them once, a total of about 5 minutes. Use a slotted spoon to remove them to a baking sheet and keep them warm in preheated oven. Repeat until all the fritters are done. Serve immediately.

VEGETABLE TERRINE WITH MOZZARELLA

Serves 8 to 10

A long list of ingredients coupled with a little extra labour may keep some from trying this impressive, colourful vegetable terrine. But it's not difficult to make and every step is worth it—even if the finished product does disappear in minutes. To make it truly vegetarian, omit the cheese. Prepare all the vegetables the day before, if you wish. Choose a Californian barrel-fermented Sauvignon Blanc for this dish.

⅓ cup (approx.)	pure olive oil	75 mL (approx.)
1	large zucchini, trimmed, cut lengthwise into thin slices	1
	salt and freshly ground black pepper	
2 tsp	chopped fresh rosemary	10 mL
1	medium eggplant, trimmed, sliced lengthwise	1
1 of each	red, yellow and orange bell pepper, oven-roasted, peeled, seeded, sliced lengthwise into 3 pieces	1 of each
1	large fennel bulb, thinly sliced	1
¾ cup + 2 tbsp	white wine	175 mL + 25 mL
1	large red onion, sliced	1
3 tbsp	chopped fresh marjoram	45 mL
1 lb	spinach, washed, dried, trimmed	500 g
¼ lb	grated Italian mozzarella	250 g
½ cup	grated Parmigiano Reggiano	125 mL
6	large plum tomatoes, fresh or canned, drained, chopped	6
4 cloves	garlic, minced	4 cloves
¼ cup	chopped fresh basil	50 mL

1. Preheat oven to 375°F (190°C). Brush a baking sheet (preferably non-stick) with a little oil. Lay the zucchini slices on the sheet, add a little salt and pepper, and sprinkle with half of the rosemary.

2. Drizzle a little oil on the zucchini and place the sheet in the oven for about 5 minutes. Turn and roast for another 5 minutes. Remove from the oven and transfer to a large platter. Wipe any burned bits off the baking sheet with a paper towel and brush it with a little more oil.

3. Repeat steps 1 and 2 (including the remaining rosemary) with the slices of eggplant, but adjusting the roasting time to about 7 minutes per side. Slices should be cooked and starting to colour when they are done. Remove them from the oven and transfer it to the platter.

4. Warm a spoonful or two of the oil in a large skillet over medium heat. Add the fennel, a little salt and pepper, and stir-fry for about 4 minutes. Add ¾ cup (175 mL) wine, cover and cook the fennel for another 5 minutes, until wine has evaporated. When cooked, transfer the fennel to the platter.

5. Wipe the skillet clean with a paper towel and return it to the heat. Warm a spoonful of the oil over medium heat; add onion slices, marjoram, a little salt and pepper, and stir to coat onion with oil and herb. Sauté for about 4 minutes. Splash in a spoonful or two of the wine and continue cooking for another 7 minutes or so, until moisture is evaporated and onions are softened. Transfer to the platter.

6. Wipe the skillet clean with a paper towel and return it to the heat. Warm a spoonful of the oil over medium heat, add spinach, a little salt and pepper, and cook quickly until all the water has evaporated and spinach has wilted. Transfer to a sieve and press the spinach against the sides with a wooden spoon to extract any water. Set aside.

7. Brush the interior of a springform pan with the remaining oil. Line with enough foil so that it hangs over the sides. Line the pan with the zucchini slices, allowing them to come up the sides of the pan and overlapping slightly, pressing them in place as you work.

8. Follow this with a layer of roasted peppers, pressing them in place. Sprinkle with a little of both cheeses.

9. Add layers of the fennel, tomatoes, onion and spinach. Sprinkle each layer with garlic, basil and the grated cheeses and press down with each addition. End with the eggplant and press down again. Fold the bits of zucchini and the edges of the foil over onto the eggplant and press again.

10. Place a heavy plate over the vegetable cake. Lay a heavy weight (a can works well) on top to help it set. Set aside for an hour or so.

11. Preheat oven to 325°F (160°C) and boil some water. Remove the plate and weight, and place the springform pan in a roasting pan. Fill it halfway

up the sides of the springform pan with boiling water. Pull out the oven rack and place the pan in the oven. Allow the terrine to heat through in the oven for about an hour.

12. Remove the pan from the oven, remove the foil from the surface and let the terrine sit for a few minutes. Place an overturned round plate over the terrine and invert it onto the plate carefully. Remove the edges of the springform pan and carefully peel off the remaining foil. Let sit for half an hour or so to settle. Using a very sharp knife, cut into wedges and serve.

ORZO WITH BLACK OLIVES, SUN-DRIED TOMATOES AND CHÈVRE

Serves 4

The pasta orzo is named by the Italians for its barley-like shape but I think it more resembles over-sized rice. This makes a nice first course served warm or at room temperature. Use good-quality sun-dried tomatoes packed in olive oil. Drain and, if they are firmer than you would like, place them in the microwave for 10 seconds or so on high to soften them.

2 tbsp	pure olive oil	25 mL
1	white onion, chopped	1
1 lb	orzo	500 g
4 cups	chicken stock	1 L
1 cup	oil-packed sun-dried tomatoes, drained, chopped	250 mL
½ cup	black olives, pitted and chopped	125 mL
2 tbsp	chopped fresh flat-leaf parsley	25 mL
¼ lb	goat cheese, crumbled	125 g

1. In a deep saucepan, warm the oil over medium heat. Add onion and cook until soft, about 5 minutes. Add the orzo and stir to coat well with the oil. Add the chicken stock. Bring to the boil, reduce heat and let simmer for about 10 minutes until just tender.

2. Remove from heat and add sun-dried tomatoes, olives and parsley. Combine well. Serve in pasta bowls with goat cheese sprinkled on top.

OYSTER JIM'S CLAYOQUOT ROASTING OYSTERS WITH CHÈVRE AND BASIL

Makes 12 appetizers

Rodney Butters, chef at The Pointe Restaurant in the truly magnificent Wickaninnish Inn in Tofino on Canada's wildly beautiful west coast, makes the most of the wealth of seafood that is available to him—almost right outside his kitchen door! Use large Pacific oysters for this lovely dish, which celebrates the briny goodness of the mollusk. Keep the shells so you can serve each oyster in one, if you wish. Choose a grassy, herbaceous Loire Valley Sauvignon Blanc as an accompaniment.

1 cup	fresh basil leaves	250 mL
2 tbsp	extra virgin olive oil	25 mL
8 oz	soft goat's cheese	250 g
12	large fresh oysters, shucked	12

1. Preheat oven broiler. Purée basil with oil in a food processor.
2. In a small bowl, blend the basil purée with goat's cheese. Spoon on top of each oyster.
3. Place oysters beneath the broiler and broil until cheese starts to melt, approximately 5 minutes. Serve immediately.

ARTICHOKE AND CHEDDAR SQUARES

Makes 16 appetizers

The chemical cynarin in artichokes lends a distinctive metallic taste to most wine, which makes it a tough match. One wine lover we know has the answer: "Serve the wine before the artichokes!" Failing that, a New Zealand Sauvignon Blanc works well.

2 (6 oz) jars	marinated artichoke hearts	160 mL
2	shallots, minced	2
2 cloves	garlic, minced	2 cloves
4	eggs, beaten	4
2 cups	grated old Cheddar cheese	500 mL
¼ tsp	salt	1 mL
⅛ tsp	cayenne	½ mL
1 tsp	hot sauce	5 mL
½ cup	grated Parmigiano Reggiano	125 mL

1. Preheat oven to 325°F (160°C). Drain artichokes well and lay them on paper towel to absorb any excess oil. Reserve the oil from one jar of artichokes. Chop artichokes finely and set to one side.

2. In a skillet, warm the reserved oil and sauté the shallots and garlic for a few minutes over medium heat. Do not allow them to brown.

3. Let mixture cool. In a mixing bowl, combine the eggs with the cheese, salt, cayenne, hot sauce and the cooled artichoke mixture. Mix well.

4. Pour this mixture into a lightly greased 11- x 7-inch (28- x 17.5-cm) baking dish. Sprinkle with Parmigiano Reggiano and bake in oven for 20 to 30 minutes. Remove from oven and let sit for 5 minutes. Cut into squares and serve warm.

CANNELLINI BEAN AND ROASTED GARLIC SALAD

Serves 4

Here is a bean salad with personality, thanks to the addition of balsamic vinegar and mellow, roasted garlic. For extra protein, texture and flavour, add some tuna packed in olive oil. Canned beans can be used if you are in a hurry—make sure to rinse and drain them well.

4 large cloves	garlic, peeled	4 large cloves
3 tbsp	extra virgin olive oil	45 mL
1-½ cups	cooked cannellini or white kidney beans	375 mL
2 tbsp	balsamic vinegar	25 mL
½ tsp	salt	2 mL
¼ tsp	freshly ground black pepper	1 mL
1 lb	mixed salad greens	500 g
½ cup	roasted red peppers, cut into strips	125 mL
¼ lb	Parmigiano Reggiano, shaved	125 g

1. Preheat oven to 325°F (160°C). Combine the garlic and oil in a small ovenproof dish; cover with foil and bake until the garlic is soft, about 30 minutes. Remove dish from oven and let it cool. Cut garlic into small pieces and add them to the beans.
2. Pour the oil from the dish into a small bowl and blend it with the balsamic vinegar, salt and pepper.
3. Toss the salad greens with a little of the roasted garlic vinaigrette. Add remaining vinaigrette to the beans; adjust seasoning, adding a little more balsamic vinegar if required.
4. Arrange greens on salad plates and distribute the beans evenly on top. Garnish with roasted red peppers and shaved Parmigiano Reggiano.

SKY-HIGH QUICHE WITH GRUYÈRE AND HAM

Serves 6 to 8

This is the quiche to serve anyone who thinks quiche is passé. It is a towering, full-bodied affair, packed with nutty Gruyère, smoky ham and the goodness of fresh eggs. Use your favourite pastry recipe or do as I did one day—use half a dozen layers of phyllo dough. It works very well and its sheer crispiness makes a nice foil to the creamy quiche. Follow the directions on the package for working with phyllo and don't omit the butter! Choose a square baking pan with the depth required to handle all the filling.

	Pastry to cover the bottom and sides of a 9-inch (2.5-L) square baking pan	
½ lb	smoked ham, thickly sliced, roughly chopped	250 g
3	green onions, trimmed, finely chopped	3
2 cups	grated Swiss Gruyère	500 mL
6	large eggs	6
¼ tsp	salt	1 mL
1 tsp	freshly ground black pepper	5 mL
½ tsp	freshly grated nutmeg	2 mL
1 cup	heavy cream	250 mL
½ cup	milk	125 mL

1. Preheat oven to 350°F (180°C). Line a baking pan with pastry, leaving a substantial overhang of about 1 inch (2.5 cm). Scatter half the ham, half the green onion and half the cheese over the bottom of the shell.
2. In a large mixing bowl, blend the eggs well with the salt, pepper and nutmeg. Add the cream, milk and the remaining ham, onion and cheese. Blend together well.
3. Place the pastry-lined baking pan on a baking sheet, open the oven and pull out the rack. Place the pan on the rack and carefully pour the quiche mixture into the pastry shell, slide the rack into the oven and bake for about 50 to 55 minutes, until it is puffed up and golden brown and a tester inserted in the centre comes out clean. Serve immediately with lightly dressed greens and ripe, sliced tomatoes.

TARRAGON CHICKEN WITH CREAM

Serves 4 to 6

So simple, yet so good, chicken in a tarragon-infused cream sauce sings with a decidedly French accent. This dish is just as pleasant at room temperature or chilled as it is hot, making it a herb- and wine-lover's favourite chicken dish in winter or summer. You can substitute the same weight in boneless chicken breasts for the whole chicken.

4 tbsp + 1 tsp	butter, softened	50 mL + 5 mL
3 tbsp	chopped fresh tarragon leaves	45 mL
	salt and freshly ground black pepper	
4 lb	roasting chicken	2 kg
½ cup	Sauvignon Blanc	125 mL
1 tsp	all-purpose flour	5 mL
¾ cup	light cream	175 mL

1. Preheat oven to 375°F (190°C). In a small bowl, blend 4 tbsp (50 mL) butter with half of the fresh tarragon and a little salt and pepper to taste. Spread a little of this mixture between the skin of the chicken and the breast meat and put the remaining herb butter in the cavity of the bird.

2. Place the chicken in a roasting pan, pour on the wine, cover and roast in the preheated oven for 1 to 1-½ hours or until chicken is thoroughly cooked through. Remove the cover for the last 15 minutes or so of cooking time, and baste with a little melted butter.

3. When it is cooked, transfer the chicken to a hot serving dish. Blend together 1 tsp (5 mL) butter and the flour. Place the roasting pan over medium-high heat and stir the butter and flour mixture into the juices in the pan, using a whisk to prevent lumps. Cook this mixture for about a minute.

4. Add cream and remaining chopped tarragon and cook gently until sauce thickens. Pour the sauce over the chicken and serve immediately, or carve the chicken and pass the tarragon sauce at the table.

PROVENÇAL SCALLOPS WITH ENDIVE

Serves 6

This is a particularly delicious and quick-to-prepare first course. It is filled with the unadulterated flavours of sweet scallops, fresh tomatoes and basil. You may want to vary the flavours once in a while by grilling the scallops instead of pan-frying them. If you do, then serve everything over freshly cooked pasta. Choose medium-sized scallops for this dish.

3	large Belgian endives, washed, trimmed	3
3 tbsp	unsalted butter	45 mL
3 cloves	garlic, minced	3 cloves
½ cup	Sauvignon Blanc	125 mL
1 tsp	salt	5 mL
½ tsp	freshly ground black pepper	2 mL
1-½ lbs	sea scallops	750 g
1 lb	fresh ripe tomatoes, peeled, seeded, chopped	500 g
1 cup	fresh basil leaves, cut into thin strips	250 mL

1. Slice each endive leaf into two and arrange on six individual serving plates. Set to one side.
2. In a large skillet, melt the butter over medium heat. Add garlic and sauté for a few seconds; don't allow it to colour.
3. Splash in the wine, salt and pepper; stir, cover and let simmer for about a minute. Add scallops and chopped tomatoes, increase heat and bring to a gentle boil, stirring and shaking the pan a little.
4. Continue cooking until scallops are cooked through, which should only take about 1-½ minutes. Just before serving, add basil.
5. Divide the mixture among the serving plates and serve immediately.

CHAPTER 9

CABERNET SAUVIGNON

Of all red grapes, Cabernet Sauvignon hits Number One on the consumer's hit parade more often than any other variety. While it has enjoyed pre-eminence as the main constituent in Bordeaux wines of the Médoc and Graves (regions on the right bank of the Gironde have mostly Merlot in their mix), it was only when California got into the act with 100 per cent Cabernet Sauvignon that adoration of this grape became a global phenomenon. Now everyone in the New World plants Cabernet, from New Zealand to Uruguay, and even in traditional wine-growing regions such as Piedmont (where Nebbiolo is king), Tuscany (Sangiovese) and Rioja (Tempranillo).

The berries of its clusters are small, which means that the ratio of skin, pits and stems to pulp is high. Since tannin is present in these parts of the grape, the tannic content of wines made from Cabernet Sauvignon is high. They taste harsh when young and take a long time to soften up, which is why they are usually blended with the fruitier Merlot even when the label suggests a single varietal wine.

In warm climates such as California, Australia and Chile, the wines are fruit-driven; they're usually treated to French or American oak, which is noticeable on the nose as a vanilla or coconut aroma in the bouquet. In cool climates such as New Zealand or Ontario, where Cabernet grapes struggle to ripen, the wines will take on herbaceous, green-pepper flavours. Even in Bordeaux you'll find in poor, wet years the wines are sinewy and lean. But at their best there is no wine better for most meat dishes. When God created lamb, He had Cabernet Sauvignon in mind.

TASTE PROFILE

Classically cedar and blackcurrant (cassis). Cooler-climate Cabernet Sauvignon wines will show more redcurrant, cranberry and pomegranate flavours, while those from warm growing regions have notes of plum and blackberries, mint or eucalyptus, and smoke.

SYNONYMS

Vidure, Bouchet, Sauvignon Rouge

BEST EXPRESSION

the classified growths of Bordeaux, Napa and Sonoma's top wineries; Chilean Reserva wines; Australia's top wineries; South Africa's top wineries (very Bordeaux in style)

SUBSTITUTES

Cabernet Franc, Merlot, Malbec

CHICKEN WITH RED PEPPERS AND ROASTED GARLIC

Serves 4

A slight variation on the classic chicken with 40 cloves of garlic, this recipe is a breeze to make and never fails to impress. The slow-roasting of the garlic alongside the chicken adds immeasurable goodness to the finished dish. Spread the soft, mellow-flavoured cloves onto warm, crusty bread and dip into the wonderful juices.

4 lb	roasting chicken	2 kg
1 tbsp	coarse salt	15 mL
1	bay leaf	1
2	heads garlic, separated, unpeeled	2
¼ cup	extra virgin olive oil	50 mL
3 sprigs	fresh rosemary	3 sprigs
2 sprigs	fresh parsley	2 sprigs
2 stalks	celery, roughly chopped	2 stalks
2	red peppers, trimmed, roughly chopped	2
	freshly ground black pepper	
1 cup	dry white wine	250 mL
1 cup	chicken stock	250 mL

1. Preheat oven to 350°F (180°C). Trim any excess fat from inside the cavity of the chicken and discard. Rub chicken with salt and place bay leaf inside the cavity.

2. In a Dutch oven, warm oil over medium heat. Add garlic, rosemary, parsley, celery, red peppers and black pepper, and sauté for 5 minutes or so. Add wine and chicken stock, bring to a boil and let simmer for 3 minutes.

3. Place chicken in the Dutch oven and turn it over a few times to coat with the mixture. Cover with a tight-fitting lid (this is important: if lid is not fitting tightly, seal edges with a paste of flour and water or with foil).

4. Bake for 1 hour. Transfer chicken to a warmed platter. Arrange vegetables around chicken. Pour juices into individual serving bowls to be enjoyed with crusty bread.

STEAK ON CIABATTA WITH STILTON BUTTER AND FRISÉE

Serves 4

A really good steak sandwich is one of life's perfect, simple pleasures. In this version, marinate the beef in the same Cabernet Sauvignon that will accompany the finished sandwich. This dish is great for summer entertaining. If you can't find frisée, use arugula or watercress or your favourite salad green.

For the marinade

½ cup	red wine	125 mL
¼ cup	extra virgin olive oil	50 mL
2 cloves	garlic, crushed	2 cloves
1	shallot, minced	1
1 tsp	herbes de Provence	5 mL
1 tbsp	balsamic vinegar	15 mL
	freshly ground black pepper	

For the dressing

4 tbsp	extra virgin olive oil	50 mL
1 tbsp	balsamic vinegar	15 mL

For the Stilton butter

¼ lb	butter, softened	125 g
¼ lb	Stilton	125 g
2 tbsp	finely chopped parsley	25 mL
1 tbsp	finely chopped chives	15 mL
	salt and freshly ground pepper	

For the sandwich

6–7 oz	sirloin tip or round steaks, ½- to ¾-inch (1- to 2-cm) thick	175–200 g
2 loaves	*ciabatta* (a flat Italian bread), halved and split lengthwise	2 loaves
½ bunch	frisée	½ bunch

1. Whisk all the marinade ingredients together. Place steaks in a shallow glass dish and pour over marinade. Turn the steaks a few times to coat them with the marinade. Cover with plastic wrap and leave for at least 2 hours (overnight is best), turning two or three times.

2. Meanwhile, place all the ingredients for the Stilton butter together in a food processor and blend until smooth. Place a sheet of waxed paper on a clean surface. Using a rubber spatula, scrape the butter onto the sheet; shape it into a cylinder and roll it up, securing either end. Chill in the refrigerator until needed.

3. When ready to grill the steak, whisk together the oil and balsamic vinegar and set it aside. Preheat grill until it is hot. Remove steaks from marinade, wipe them with paper towels, season with a little salt and pepper, and grill for 2 to 3 minutes on each side or longer if you like steak well done.

4. Warm ciabatta on the grill while steaks are cooking. Toss the salad greens together with a little of the dressing until leaves are coated.

5. Remove ciabatta from the grill and brush each half with remaining dressing. Arrange frisée on the bottom halves of bread and top each with a steak. Add a slice of Stilton butter to each steak and arrange the top of the bread alongside before serving.

SPICY SPARERIB STEW

Serves 4 to 6

Plan to make these ribs at least one day before serving. Reason one: it is an effortless job to remove the fat from the surface once the liquid has been left to sit overnight. Reason two: the taste is improved immeasurably. These may be the best ribs you'll ever make. Ask your butcher to cut crosswise through the bone into strips just over an inch (2.5 cm) wide to cut down on your preparation time. Look for salted black beans in Chinese or Asian supermarkets or in the specialty section of large supermarkets.

4 lbs	lean spareribs	2 kg
⅓ cup	salted black beans	75 mL
1 tbsp	chopped gingerroot	15 mL
1 head	garlic, separated, cloves peeled and smashed	1 head
¼ cup	light soy sauce	50 mL
1 tbsp	light brown sugar	15 mL
4	whole peppercorns	4
1 cup	Cabernet Sauvignon	250 mL
½ cup	water	125 mL
3 tbsp	vegetable oil	45 mL
1 tsp	dried red pepper flakes	5 mL
3	green onions, chopped	3

1. If necessary, trim the spareribs of excess fat. In a small saucepan, over medium heat, combine the beans, gingerroot, garlic, soy sauce, brown sugar, peppercorns, Cabernet Sauvignon and water, stirring to dissolve the sugar. Remove from heat and set to one side.

2. In a large, heavy pot, warm the oil over high heat. Reduce heat and add pepper flakes and green onions. Sauté briefly, then add the ribs and toss together until the meat browns, about 5 minutes.

3. Add the contents of the small saucepan, bring to the boil and immediately reduce heat to a simmer. Cover and let simmer for between 1 and 1-½ hours until ribs are quite tender, stirring occasionally.

4. Transfer the ribs to a bowl; let cool, cover with plastic wrap and refrigerate overnight. Let liquids cool somewhat, then cover and refrigerate. Skim the excess fat from the liquids and discard.

5. Return the pot to medium heat, add ribs and heat them through. Serve with steamed rice and thinly sliced cucumber in a light vinaigrette.

LINGUINE WITH FAVA BEANS

Serves 6

A Cabernet Franc makes a nice companion to this combination of pasta and fresh beans. Fresh young fava beans (or, as the English call them, broad beans) do not need their individual husks or skins peeled; if they look as though they do, they are too old—period. However, there are those who maintain that the inner skin of each bean should be removed. Clearly, it is a matter of personal taste.

3 tbsp	pure olive oil	45 mL
1	red onion, thinly sliced	1
1 lb	shelled fresh young tender fava beans (or broad beans)	500 g
¾ cup	vegetable broth (or light chicken broth)	175 mL
	salt and freshly ground black pepper	
1 tsp	coarse salt	5 mL
1 lb	linguine	500 g
1 tbsp	butter	15 mL
8–10 leaves	fresh basil, roughly chopped	8–10 leaves
1 cup	grated Parmigiano Reggiano	250 mL

1. In a heavy skillet, warm the oil over medium heat and sauté the onion for 10 minutes, until softened. Add beans and broth, and season to taste with salt and pepper. Increase the heat and bring to a boil; cover, reduce the heat to medium and allow the beans to cook for about 15 to 20 minutes, until they are tender.
2. Bring a large pot of water to the boil and add coarse salt. Cook the pasta until it is tender but firm; drain and return it to the pot. Add the contents of the skillet, the butter and salt and pepper, along with the chopped basil and half of the grated Parmigiano Reggiano. Toss well.
3. Transfer to a warmed serving bowl. Sprinkle the remaining grated cheese over the top and serve immediately.

ENGLISH COTTAGE PIE

Serves 4 to 6

To the unschooled North American, a traditional cottage pie may seem much like a shepherd's pie, both being combinations of ground meat topped with mashed potatoes. There is an important distinction between the two, however. Authentic shepherd's pie is traditionally made with lamb—not beef—and is generally made with leftover roast lamb, chopped fine and blended with that roast's gravy. Cottage pie is always made with good-quality ground beef—or mince, as the English call it—combined with a handful of ingredients to bring out all its savoury goodness. Simple, good comforting food at its best.

2 tbsp	olive oil	25 mL
1	large onion, chopped	1
1	large carrot, diced	1
2 cloves	garlic, chopped	2 cloves
1-½ lbs	lean ground beef	750 g
2 cups	chopped tomatoes (fresh or canned)	500 mL
3 tbsp	tomato paste	45 mL
2 tsp	Worcestershire sauce	10 mL
	salt and freshly ground black pepper	
1-¼ cups	water	300 mL
1-½ lbs	baking potatoes, peeled, quartered	750 g
3 tbsp	butter	45 mL
⅔–1-¼ cups	whole milk	150-300 mL

1. In a large heavy skillet over medium heat, warm the oil and sauté the onion, carrot and garlic until softened and lightly coloured. Increase the heat and add half of the ground beef. Sauté, breaking the meat up as it cooks. When lightly browned, using a slotted spoon, transfer to a bowl.

2. Add remaining ground beef to the pan and repeat the procedure. Add the first batch of beef to the skillet along with the tomatoes, tomato paste, Worcestershire sauce, salt and pepper. Stir in the water.

3. Bring to the boil, reduce heat and simmer gently, stirring occasionally, for about an hour, adding a little more hot water if needed. Halfway through the simmering, cover loosely with a lid.

4. Preheat oven to 400°F (200°C). Cook the potatoes in a pot of boiling water to which you have added a little salt. Drain and mash well. When they are half mashed, add butter, milk, and salt and pepper to taste. Continue mashing and then beat two or three times with a wooden spoon.

5. To assemble, transfer the meat mixture to a pie dish or similar ovenproof dish. Top with mashed potatoes and smooth the surface. Dot with a little butter and bake until heated through and the potatoes are beginning to get golden brown, about 30 minutes.

SAUSAGES AND ONIONS IN RED WINE

Serves 4

Choose a Cabernet Franc for this solid, satisfying recipe that begs to be accompanied by a rich potato gratin. Pass a strong mustard at the table to accompany the sausages.

2 tbsp	unsalted butter	25 mL
8–10	large butcher-quality pork or beef sausages	8–10
1	large white onion, sliced	1
1 cup	Cabernet Franc or Cabernet Sauvignon	250 mL
	salt and freshly ground black pepper	

1. In a large skillet, melt the butter. Sauté the sausages for a few minutes until they begin to brown all over. Preheat oven to 375°F (190°C).

2. Using tongs, transfer the sausages to an ovenproof dish large enough to accommodate them in one layer. Return the skillet to the heat, add a little more butter if necessary and sauté the onion slices until they are brown, about 10 minutes.

3. Pour the wine into the skillet over the onions, scraping up any bits of onion and sausage that are clinging to the bottom. Bring mixture to the boil and then pour it over sausages. Add a little salt and pepper, cover and bake for about half an hour.

BOLLITO MISTO WITH SALSA VERDE

Serves 6

The classic *bollito misto* (boiled mixed meats) is a big, generous labour-intensive affair with a number of different meats including beef, chicken, cotechino sausage, lamb or veal tongue, and even calf's foot or ox's tail. Reminiscent of a down-east "boiled dinner" or a sturdy French *pot au feu,* it is a straightforward dish that is not at all hard to make—but it does take a bit of time. This version is streamlined for contemporary tastes and combines a beef brisket with a whole boneless chicken breast and a colourful collection of vegetables. In Tuscany, it is served with *salsa verde*—green sauce—and it contributes immeasurably toward the success of this much anticipated meal. Make the *salsa verde* first or while the meat and vegetables are cooking.

3 lbs	beef brisket (or other cut of beef suitable for boiling)	1.5 kg
8 cups	cold water	2 L
1 lb	beef marrow bone (about 3 pieces)	500 g
6	carrots, chopped	6
3	leeks, trimmed, halved, washed, chopped	3
6 stalks	celery, chopped	6 stalks
6	baby or small onions, peeled, left whole	6
1	whole boneless chicken breast	1
¼	large Savoy cabbage, core removed, cut into wedges	¼
	salt and freshly ground black pepper	
	beef extract, optional	

1. Place the beef brisket in a large Dutch oven or heavy saucepan. Cover with water and add beef bones.
2. Cover with a lid and bring to a boil over high heat. When it has come to the boil, reduce heat to low and cook gently for 2-½ hours.
3. Remove brisket to a platter and cover it with foil. Discard bones. Pour off any excess fat from the stock. Add carrots, leeks, celery and onion to the pot and cook for another 10 minutes. Add chicken breast and simmer for 5 minutes or until it is cooked through.
4. Add cabbage and cook for another 5 minutes. Season to taste.

5. When the vegetables are tender, remove the pot from the heat. Use tongs to remove the chicken and vegetables to a warmed bowl. Return the pot to the heat so that the stock gently simmers. Adjust the seasoning and add a little beef extract if necessary.

6. Meanwhile, transfer the beef and chicken to a cutting board and slice meat into diagonal 1-inch (2.5-cm) slices. Arrange them on serving platter with vegetables. Spoon some of the broth over top and serve. Serve the remaining hot broth at the table along with the *salsa verde.*

SALSA VERDE

Makes about 1-½cups (375 mL)

1 slice	rustic country-style Italian bread	1 slice
3 tbsp	red wine vinegar	45 mL
1-½ cups	roughly chopped flat-leaf parsley	375 mL
2 cloves	garlic, peeled, halved	2 cloves
1	hard-boiled egg yolk	1
1 tbsp	capers, drained	15 mL
	salt and freshly ground black pepper to taste	
1 cup	extra virgin olive oil	250 mL

1. In a small bowl, soak the bread in the vinegar for about 10 minutes. Drain and squeeze bread dry. Reserve vinegar.

2. In a food processor or blender, combine bread, parsley, garlic, egg yolk, capers, salt and pepper. With the machine running, add oil in a thin stream until mixture thickens to a sauce-like consistency.

3. Add vinegar and blend well. Serve at room temperature.

MOUSSAKA

Serves 6

You will find this moussaka recipe far less oily than you may be used to. This is because the eggplant is baked, not fried, before it is combined with other ingredients. *Kefalotyri* cheese is a hard, salty cheese for grating made from sheep or goat's milk. If you cannot obtain it, substitute Italian pecorino romano.

3 tbsp	olive oil	45 mL
1	large onion, chopped	1
2 cloves	garlic, chopped	2 cloves
1 lb	lean ground lamb (or beef)	500 g
2 tbsp	tomato paste	25 mL
1 cup	Cabernet Sauvignon	250 mL
4 cups	canned plum tomatoes, roughly chopped	1 L
1 tsp	sugar	5 mL
1-½ tsp	cinnamon	7 mL
	salt and freshly ground black pepper	
2 tsp	chopped fresh oregano	10 mL
3 tbsp	chopped fresh parsley	45 mL
3	large eggplant	3
2 tbsp	butter	25 mL
2 tbsp	all-purpose flour	25 mL
2-⅓ cups	milk	575 mL
¼ tsp	freshly grated nutmeg	1 mL
6 oz	grated kefalotyri cheese	160 g
1	egg	1
1	egg yolk	1
½ tsp	cinnamon	2 mL

1. In a large skillet, warm the oil over medium-high heat. Sauté the onion and garlic until softened and pale golden, about 3 to 4 minutes. Add ground lamb and continue to sauté until it is gently cooked.

2. Dissolve tomato paste in the wine and add to the meat along with the tomatoes, sugar and cinnamon. Season to taste. Mix to combine well and bring to a gentle boil. Reduce heat immediately to low to allow meat sauce to simmer and thicken, about 30 minutes. Stir in oregano and parsley. Set aside.

3. Trim and slice the eggplant lengthwise. Transfer slices to a colander or a counter lined with paper towel. Sprinkle slices with a little salt and leave for at least half an hour to drain. Preheat oven to 375°F (190°C). Pat slices dry with paper towel and lay them on an oiled baking sheet. Bake slices for 15 to 20 minutes until they are softened and beginning to brown.

4. Melt the butter in a medium-sized saucepan over medium-high heat. Blend in the flour with a whisk, cooking and whisking for a minute to allow flour to lose its raw taste. Reduce heat to very low and add milk gradually, whisking as you do so until all the milk has been incorporated. Allow mixture to cook over a gentle heat until it is thick. Remove pan from heat and add nutmeg, half the grated cheese, a little salt and pepper, and blend well until cheese is melted. Set aside.

5. Lightly oil a 13- x 9-inch (33- x 23-cm) rectangular baking dish. Place half the eggplant slices on the bottom (they may overlap), and distribute half the meat sauce over them. Repeat this procedure with the remaining eggplant and meat sauce.

6. Preheat oven to 350°F (160° C). Add the egg and the egg yolk to the white sauce, whisking to blend well. Use a large spoon to spread the white sauce over the surface of the meat sauce. Sprinkle the remaining grated cheese and the cinnamon on top. Let it sit for a few minutes, then bake for 1 hour until the surface is deep golden brown. Remove from oven and let sit for 10 minutes before serving.

BISTRO STEAKS WITH MUSTARD CREAM

Serves 6

This recipe, a popular bistro dish, also works well with fresh boneless pork steaks, which are available at good butchers.

6	strip or rib-eye steaks, 1-¼-inches (8-cm) thick	6
¼ cup	olive oil	50 mL
	salt and freshly ground black pepper	
⅔ cup	cognac or brandy	150 mL
1-½ cups	beef broth	375 mL
2–3 tbsp	cold butter	25–45 mL
⅓ cup	heavy cream	75 mL
3 tbsp	Dijon mustard	45 mL
	freshly chopped parsley for garnish	

1. Pat the steaks dry with a paper towel. Rub the surfaces of the steaks with the oil, making sure to rub it in well. Then sprinkle meat generously with salt and pepper.

2. Place a heavy frying pan over medium-high heat and allow it to get quite hot. Sear the steaks for about 5 seconds on each side. Reduce heat to medium and cook to your taste (about 4 minutes on each side for medium). Transfer steaks to a warm platter.

3. Splash the cognac or brandy into the hot pan, scraping the bottom of the pan to loosen any bits of meat. Cook for a minute to evaporate the alcohol, then add beef broth. Continue to cook at a relatively high heat to reduce liquid by one third. Reduce heat to medium.

4. Add butter in pieces and stir to blend into the sauce. Add cream and mustard. Whisk together and continue to cook until all ingredients are well blended and sauce is thickened.

5. Pour sauce over steaks and sprinkle them with chopped parsley. Serve immediately with mashed potatoes and crisp, lightly dressed greens.

CHAPTER 10

PINOT NOIR

Any wine grower will tell you that Pinot Noir is both a blessing and a curse—rather like the little girl with the curl: when she is good, she is very, very good, but when she's bad she's horrid. It is the most difficult grape to capture at its peak of ripeness: picked too early, its flavours are green; allowed to ripen fully, it can turn into cooked raspberry jam. Even in Burgundy, its spiritual home, Pinot Noir is a hit-and-miss affair, which is very frustrating for consumers because the wines are generally on the expensive side. But at its finest, Pinot Noir is the greatest wine experience you'll ever have.

Few regions outside Burgundy can grow Pinot Noir successfully. Oregon has consistently made good Pinot Noir in the New World. Some California producers such as Calera, Mondavi and Saintsbury make good products but generally California is too warm for the fickle Pinot Noir grape. There are also notable successes in the cooler regions of Australia, namely Tasmania. New Zealand also produces very fine Pinot Noir in Martinborough and Central Otago. Occasionally, Alsace and Germany can make commendable Pinot Noir, as can Ontario and New York—but it takes late fall sunshine and long dry spells leading up to harvest. Its most bizarre representation is in Bouzy Rouge, the red wine of a Champagne village; Pinot Noir fermented as a white wine (no contact with the grape skin) is a constituent of most champagnes—so even if it doesn't ripen as a red wine in cool climates, it has its uses in sparkling wines.

TASTE PROFILE

Raspberries, violets, sometimes strawberries. In warm climates more cherry to black cherry and a range of bouquets that can include rust, tomato, gamey-animal smells and what Burgundians refer to as "barnyard" aromas.

SYNONYMS

Pinot Nero (Italy), Spätburgunder, Blauburgunder (Germany), Nagyburgundi (Hungary)

BEST EXPRESSION

top wines of Burgundy's Côte de Beaune (medium-bodied) and Côte de Nuits (fuller-bodied), top Oregon wineries, some producers in California—Calera and some producers in the Carneros region, such as Mondavi, Acacia, Saintsbury; Australia's Yarra Valley and Tasmania; New Zealand (Martinborough)

SUBSTITUTES

named Beaujolais village wines, Valpolicella, Barbera

GRILLED PORTOBELLO MUSHROOMS ON ARUGULA

Serves 6

If you prefer, you can combine portobello mushrooms with a few oyster mushrooms and chanterelles in this recipe, which makes a very nice first course.

2 tsp	balsamic vinegar	10 mL
2 cloves	garlic, minced	2 cloves
2 tsp	chopped fresh rosemary	10 mL
¼ cup	extra virgin olive oil	50 mL
1-½ lbs	portobello mushrooms, stemmed (or an assortment as described above)	750 g
	salt and freshly ground black pepper	
4 cups	arugula	1 L

For the vinaigrette

1 tbsp	Dijon mustard	15 mL
2 tbsp	lemon juice	25 mL
¼ cup	extra virgin olive oil	50 mL
	salt and freshly ground black pepper	
¼ lb	Parmigiano Reggiano, shaved	125 g

1. Preheat grill. In a medium-sized mixing bowl, combine the vinegar, garlic, rosemary and oil. Toss the mushrooms in this mixture until they are well-coated. Season with salt and pepper. Grill mushrooms on a hot grill until softened (if using smaller mushrooms, a grill basket may be required).
2. Wash, trim and dry the arugula and place it in a large mixing bowl. In a small bowl, whisk together the mustard, lemon juice, oil, salt and pepper. Add vinaigrette to greens and toss to coat well.
3. To serve, arrange dressed greens on serving plates, top with grilled mushrooms and garnish with a few curls of Parmigiano Reggiano. Serve immediately.

PORCINI AND SAUSAGE RISOTTO

Serves 6

Just the thing for a cold wintry night, this sumptuous risotto relies on good-quality dried porcini and the best, leanest Italian sausage you can find to make it truly great. Luganega, a sausage that is a specialty of Northern Italy, is a perfect choice if available.

2 oz	dried porcini mushrooms	50 g
6 cups	quality chicken broth (approximate)	1.5 L
2 tbsp	extra virgin olive oil	25 mL
2 tbsp	butter	25 mL
1	onion, finely chopped	1
2 cloves	garlic, minced	2 cloves
½ lb	Italian sausage, cut into ½-inch (1-cm) pieces	250 g
2 cups	short-grained Italian arborio rice	500 mL
½ cup	Pinot Noir	125 mL
½ cup	grated Parmigiano Reggiano	125 mL
	salt and freshly ground black pepper	

1. In a bowl, combine porcini mushrooms with warm water to cover; let stand 30 minutes. Drain. Rinse mushrooms, chop roughly and set them aside. Pour soaking liquid through a cheesecloth-lined sieve and reserve.
2. In a large saucepan, bring chicken broth to a boil. Reduce heat to a slow simmer and keep the liquid at this steady, slightly bubbling level throughout the rest of the cooking.
3. In a heavy-bottomed saucepan, heat oil and butter over medium-high heat. Add onion and cook for 2 minutes or until translucent. Add garlic and cook for another 2 minutes. Add sausage pieces and sauté until sausage is browned.
4. Add rice and porcini and stir for a minute or two, or until grains are well coated with butter and oil. Add wine and the reserved mushroom liquid, and stir until most of the liquid has been absorbed.
5. Using a ladle, add simmering broth ½ cup (125 mL) at a time. As each ladle of broth is added, stir the rice to keep it from sticking to the bottom

and sides of the saucepan; do not add more broth until last addition has been absorbed.

6. Repeat this process, ladling in the hot broth and stirring, for 15 minutes or so. If the stock is absorbed too quickly, reduce the heat to maintain a low, steady simmer. As you near the end of the cooking time, reduce the amount of broth to ¼ cup (50 mL) at a time.

7. Continue to cook, adding more broth as necessary, until the rice is tender but with a firm heart and overall creaminess. A minute before completion, stir in the grated cheese and season to taste. Serve immediately.

PORK LOIN AL LATTE

Serves 4 to 6

This is a very old Italian method for braising pork that ensures succulent meat every time.

2-½ lbs	boneless loin of pork	1.25 kg
3 cloves	garlic, chopped	3 cloves
1	large carrot, finely chopped	1
1	celery stalk, finely chopped	1
1	onion, finely chopped	1
4 cups	whole milk	1 L
⅓ cup	dry white wine	75 mL
	salt and freshly ground black pepper	

1. Place the pork, garlic, carrot, celery and onion into a Dutch oven or heavy ovenproof casserole. Pour milk over everything, bring to a boil, then reduce heat to medium so that the milk is just bubbling. Cook for about an hour, loosely covered, turning pork occasionally.

2. Remove meat from casserole, transfer to a warmed platter and cover with foil. Increase heat and start reducing sauce. Cook sauce until it is thickened and brown; strain it through a sieve.

3. Return sauce to pan, add wine and stir, scraping up bits from bottom of pan. When sauce is thickened and brown, season with salt and pepper. Carve pork into slices and spoon sauce over.

STUFFED PORK CHOPS WITH MUSHROOM CREAM GRAVY

Serves 4 to 6

Decidedly old-fashioned, and deservedly great because of it, this dish will please everyone from the meat-and-spud fan to the fussiest gourmand. Vary the stuffing from time to time with bits of apple or pear or dried apricot and raisins.

2 tbsp	butter	25 mL
1	medium onion, chopped	1
1 cup	chopped mushrooms	250 mL
1 cup	small bread cubes	250 mL
1 tbsp	chopped fresh parsley	15 mL
¼ tsp	salt	1 mL
2 tsp	chopped fresh thyme	10 mL
2 tsp	chopped fresh sage	10 mL
	freshly ground black pepper	
1	egg, lightly beaten	1
4	extra thick pork chops (ask the butcher to cut pockets in each)	4
½ cup	Pinot Noir	125 mL

For the Mushroom Cream Gravy

	pan drippings	
2 tbsp	all-purpose flour	25 mL
1 cup	light beef broth	250 mL
½ cup	Pinot Noir	125 mL
1 cup	thinly sliced mushrooms	250 mL
½ cup	sour cream	125 mL
	salt and freshly ground black pepper	

1. Preheat oven to 350°F (180°C). In a large skillet, heat the butter over medium-high heat. Sauté the onion until pale golden, about 3 minutes. Add

mushrooms and cook, stirring occasionally, for about 2 minutes. Transfer mixture to a mixing bowl.

2. Add bread cubes, parsley, salt, fresh thyme, sage and pepper. Mix well with your hands, then add beaten egg and mix again to incorporate all the ingredients.

3. Stuff the pork chops with this mixture and secure with either butcher's twine or toothpicks. Arrange the chops on a rack in a roasting pan. Place on the shelf of the oven, then pour Pinot Noir over chops. Cover tightly with foil and bake for about half an hour. Remove the foil, add a little more wine if necessary, and continue to bake for another 10 to 15 minutes or so, until pork is cooked through. Transfer the pork to a serving platter and keep warm while preparing the gravy.

4. Pour the drippings from the pan into a bowl. Set the roasting pan over medium-high heat and scrape up any bits clinging to the bottom. Blend in the flour and cook for a minute or two. Gradually add the drippings to the flour, whisking as you do so to prevent lumps. Slowly whisk in the beef broth and then the wine, blending all the while. Bring to a gentle boil, reduce heat and let simmer, stirring, until thickened.

5. Add sliced mushrooms and simmer for another 5 minutes or so. Stir in sour cream, salt and pepper, and let simmer for another few minutes until thickened and well blended. When piping hot, pour over pork chops and serve immediately.

CHICKEN BREASTS WITH TRUFFLE AND FONTINA

Serves 6

Reserve this elegant dish for a special occasion. If you cannot locate—or your budget won't allow—white or black truffles, substitute some sliced wild mushrooms drizzled with a little truffle oil. Truffle oil is olive oil infused with truffle and is available wherever good-quality Italian foodstuffs are sold or at specialty food shops.

6	boneless, skinless chicken breasts	6
	salt and freshly ground black pepper	
	all-purpose flour as needed for dredging	
2 tbsp	butter	25 mL
2 tbsp	olive oil	25 mL
36	thin slices of white or black truffle	36
6 slices	Italian fontina cheese	6 slices

1. Place chicken breasts between sheets of waxed paper and pound gently until they are a uniform thinness.
2. Sprinkle with salt and pepper, and dip them in flour to cover both sides, shaking off any excess. Combine butter and oil in a large skillet over medium-high heat. Place chicken breasts in the pan, three at a time, and cook until they are tender, about 5 to 6 minutes per side. Preheat broiler.
3. Transfer chicken breasts to a small roasting pan and add a little more salt and pepper. Arrange slices of truffle on each breast and cover each with a slice of fontina.
4. Slip beneath a preheated broiler until cheese melts and is slightly bubbly. Serve immediately.

CHAPTER 11
SHIRAZ/SYRAH

Syrah is an under-appreciated grape in France, playing second fiddle to Cabernet Sauvignon, Merlot and Pinot Noir. It makes the great wines of the Northern Rhône—Hermitage and Côte Rôtie, which can age for many years; it is also a constituent in the blends of the Southern Rhône reds, such as Châteauneuf-du-Pape, where Grenache is the predominant grape. Don't confuse Syrah with Petite Sirah grown in California, which is another variety (the French call it Durif). This grape is also widely planted in the Midi, where the wines have improved greatly since the mid-1980s.

The Australians and South Africans call the Syrah grape Shiraz and use it extensively as a blending wine with Cabernet Sauvignon, although some of Australia's finest wines (notably Grange) are made exclusively from Shiraz.

TASTE PROFILE

Syrah makes a full-bodied wine that tends to be deeply coloured with a bouquet of blackberry and smoke, tar or iodine. The wine is fleshy with a good fruit flavour—blackberries and freshly ground white or black pepper. Like Cabernet Sauvignon, it is high in tannin and requires a few years of bottle age to soften. Australian Shiraz tends to be jammier and softer than the Syrah of the Northern Rhône.

SYNONYMS

Schiras, Sirah, Petite Syrah (but not Petite Sirah), Marsanne Noir

BEST EXPRESSION

the wines of the Northern Rhône (Hermitage, Côte Rôtie, Cornas, St. Joseph and Crozes-Hermitage), especially producers such as Guigal, Vidal-Fleurie, Jaboulet, Chapoutier; from Australia, Grange, Eileen Hardy; Nichol Vineyards in British Columbia does a first-rate job with this variety

SUBSTITUTES

Zinfandel, Amarone, Barolo

EIGENSINN FARM BRAISED BEEF SHANK

Serves 4

Chef Michael Stadtländer devised this sturdy, aromatic dish for a Second Harvest fund-raiser. At the event, he served the succulent, braised beef piled high on slices of sourdough bread—and it makes a great appetizer that way. Or serve it at the table with mashed potatoes to catch the beautifully flavoured sauce.

2 tbsp	olive oil	25 mL
4	beef shanks, about 10 oz (300 g) each	4
2 cups	beef broth	500 mL
2 cups	tomatoes, fresh or canned, puréed	500 mL
1 tbsp	chopped fresh rosemary	15 mL
1 tbsp	juniper berries	15 mL
2 tsp	peppercorns	10 mL
2 cloves	garlic, minced	2 cloves
4 thick slices	sourdough bread	4 thick slices

1. In saucepan, heat oil over high heat. Brown meat on all sides. Transfer the beef shanks to a large stock pot along with broth, tomatoes, rosemary, juniper berries, peppercorns and garlic. Bring to a boil.

2. Reduce heat and simmer for 4 to 5 hours or until meat is tender and beginning to fall from the bone.

3. Serve beef with the sauce on slices of sourdough bread or as described above.

MOROCCAN LENTIL SOUP COUILLARD

Serves 4 to 6

Toronto-based chef Greg Couillard of the restaurant Sarkis is renowned for his way with spices, exotic herbs, fruits and vegetables and his thoroughly unique cooking style. Here is his recipe for a vibrantly flavoured soup that may change forever the way you feel about the humble lentil.

2 cups	brown lentils, rinsed	500 mL
10 cups	water	2.5 L
2 tbsp	olive oil	25 mL
2	onions, chopped	2
4 cloves	garlic, minced	4 cloves
1	red bell pepper, seeded and chopped	1
1	large carrot, chopped	1
1 stalk	celery, chopped	1 stalk
4	bay leaves	4
1	cinnamon stick	1
1 tsp	hot curry powder	5 mL
1 tsp	ground cumin	5 mL
1	whole chile pepper	1
2 cups	tomato sauce	500 mL
2 cups	chopped assorted fall vegetables (a combinationof white turnip, squash, yams, spinach, kale, Swiss chard or your choice)	500 mL
4 cups	chicken broth	1 L
	salt and freshly ground black pepper	

1. In a large saucepan, add lentils to 10 cups of water, set over high heat and bring to a boil. Reduce heat and simmer for 25 minutes. Drain and reserve the cooking liquid.

2. In a large soup pot, warm the oil over medium-high heat. Sauté the onion and garlic with a little salt for about 10 minutes, stirring. Add red pepper, carrot, celery, bay leaves and cinnamon stick, and continue to sauté for 3 minutes, stirring.

3. Add curry powder, cumin and chile pepper, and stir to combine well. Stir in lentils, tomato sauce and the vegetables. Add chicken broth and enough of the reserved lentil cooking liquid to cover everything by half an inch (1 cm) of liquid.

4. Bring to a boil, reduce heat to a simmer and simmer for 30 minutes, until vegetables are tender. Adjust seasoning and serve immediately with lots of crusty bread.

VENISON AGRODOLCE

Serves 6

Italians like to treat stronger flavoured meats to this sweet and sour sauce based on vinegar and a little sugar. Today farm-raised game means a gentler, milder tasting meat but the method still works well to complement venison or lamb. Because farm-raised venison is so lean, it needs the additional fat provided by the pancetta. If using lamb, omit it.

2 tbsp	pure olive oil	25 mL
¼ lb	pancetta, chopped	125 g
3 lbs	venison, cut into 1-inch (2.5-cm) cubes	1.5 kg
	salt and freshly ground black pepper	
¼ cup	tomato paste	50 mL
4 cups	beef broth	1 L
1 cup	balsamic vinegar	250 mL
3 tsp	sugar	15 mL

1. In a large skillet or Dutch oven, heat the oil and sauté pancetta for 5 minutes, until it is almost crisp. Season venison with salt and pepper and add it, in batches, to skillet to brown on all sides.

2. Dissolve tomato paste in broth and add to skillet with vinegar and sugar. Bring to a boil, reduce heat to low and cook, covered for about 2-½ to 3 hours, until venison is tender and sauce is thickened. Serve with mashed potatoes and rapini or spinach sautéed with a little olive oil and garlic.

TOURTIÈRE WITH RED ONION CONFIT

Serves 6 to 8

Quebec's classic pork pie needs little in the way of embellishment. Yet this accompanying onion marmalade works remarkably well with it, as would a chunky homemade apple sauce treated with a little cinnamon and freshly grated nutmeg.

1 lb	ground pork	500 g
½ lb	ground veal	250 g
1	medium onion, chopped	1
1 large clove	garlic, finely chopped	1 large clove
1-½ tsp	salt	7 mL
1 tsp	freshly ground black pepper	5 mL
¼ tsp	cloves	1 mL
½ tsp	freshly grated nutmeg	2 mL
1 cup	water	250 mL
1 slice	white bread, cubed	1 slice

For the pastry

1-½ cups	all-purpose flour	375 mL
½ tsp	salt	2 mL
½ cup	shortening (in Quebec, lard is the preferred choice)	125 mL
3–4 tbsp	ice water	45–50 mL
	milk for brushing	

1. In a large saucepan, combine the pork and veal with the onion, garlic, salt, pepper, cloves, nutmeg and water. Bring to a gentle boil, stirring to blend all the ingredients, then reduce heat to a simmer. Cook for 20 minutes. Remove from heat and stir in the bread cubes. Adjust seasoning. Set aside.

2. To make the pastry, in a mixing bowl combine the flour with the salt. Cut in the shortening or lard with a fork or pastry blender until the mixture begins to look crumbly. Stir in the ice water, a little at a time, until you can gather pastry in a ball in your hands.

3. On a floured board, roll two-thirds of the pastry to fit a 9-inch (23-cm) pie plate. Preheat oven to 400°F (200°C). Pour the meat mixture into the pastry shell and spread it out evenly. Roll out the remaining pastry and use it to cover the top. Pinch the edges of the pastry together and trim. Cut slits in the top to allow steam to escape and brush with a little milk to help it to brown. Bake for 45 to 55 minutes. Serve with red onion confit (recipe follows).

RED ONION CONFIT

Makes about 1-½ cups

Delightful with sausages and omelettes, in sandwiches, with cold meats and cheese, and alongside any pork dish.

2 tbsp	butter	25 mL
2 tbsp	extra virgin olive oil	25 mL
½ cup	sugar	125 mL
1-½ lbs	red onions, thinly sliced	750 g
¾ cup	red wine	175 mL
⅓ cup + 1 tbsp	red wine vinegar	75 mL + 15 mL

1. In a large saucepan, melt the butter in the oil over low heat. Add sugar and stir to dissolve completely. Add the onions all at once; stir to cover with butter and sugar mixture. Cover loosely and cook about 30 minutes, stirring occasionally.

2. Stir in wine and vinegar and increase heat to bring to a boil. Reduce heat and simmer gently, uncovered, for another 30 minutes.

3. Increase heat once more and cook, stirring, 5 to 8 minutes, or until mixture becomes thick and jam-like. Remove from heat and allow to cool. Pack into a sterilized jar and store in the refrigerator for up to a month.

GRILLED LAMB TENDERLOIN WITH PEPPERONATA BUCHANAN

Serves 6

This is a variation on a wonderful dish invented by Toronto-based chef Robert Buchanan of Acqua Ristorante for a fund-raiser for Second Harvest a few years back. At the event, Chef Buchanan served it with a full-flavoured pepper relish.

For the pepperonata

1	red bell pepper, roasted, peeled, cut into strips	1
1	yellow bell pepper, roasted, peeled, cut into strips	1
½ cup	extra virgin olive oil	125 mL
¼ cup	fresh basil leaves, cut into thin strips	50 mL
2 cloves	garlic, minced	2 cloves
1	jalapeño, minced	1
1 tbsp	capers, drained	15 mL
	salt and freshly ground black pepper	

For the lamb

6	lamb tenderloins	6
¼ cup	extra virgin olive oil	50 mL
1 clove	garlic, minced	1 clove
	salt and freshly ground black pepper	
1 large handful	enoki mushrooms	1 large handful
1 bunch	arugula, washed, trimmed, dried	1 bunch
	fresh chives for tying	

1. To make the pepperonata, in a mixing bowl combine the red and yellow pepper strips with the oil, basil, garlic, jalapeño and capers. Season to taste and set aside.

2. To make the lamb, preheat grill to medium-high. Rub lamb with oil and garlic; sprinkle it with salt and pepper. Grill about 2 minutes, turning, or until medium-rare. Let cool slightly.

3. To assemble, wrap each lamb tenderloin and some enoki mushroom in a few arugula leaves and bind with a couple of strands of chive. Serve with pepperonata.

DUCK BREAST RAGOÛT

Serves 4 to 6

Perfect for a late fall supper, this rich, hearty duck stew gets its goodness from the new world Shiraz in which it is cooked, plus the combination of bacon, leeks and mushrooms. Serve with mounds of Yukon Gold mashed potatoes and steamed wedges of brilliant green cabbage drizzled with butter.

½ bottle	Shiraz	½ bottle
2-½ cups	strong chicken broth	625 mL
2 tbsp	butter	25 mL
2 tbsp	olive oil	25 mL
4	boneless duck breasts	4
¼ lb	quality bacon, chopped	125 g
1	leek, trimmed, rinsed well and cut into fine strips	1
2	shallots, minced	2
¼ lb	brown cremini mushrooms	125 g
	salt and freshly ground black pepper	

1. In a large saucepan, combine the Shiraz and chicken broth over medium-high heat, bring to a gentle boil and allow to reduce to one third of its original volume.

2. While the liquid is reducing, in a large skillet melt the butter with the oil over high heat. Add duck breasts and pan-fry about 10 minutes in total, turning once. The duck should not be totally cooked.

3. Transfer the duck to a plate to cool slightly. Then pull off and discard the skin and cut each breast into six pieces. Set it aside.

4. In the same skillet, sauté the bacon, leek, shallots and mushrooms for about 10 minutes, stirring until cooked through. Pour off bacon fat. Add some of the wine reduction to the pan, scrape up any bits remaining, and then transfer the contents of the pan to the saucepan containing the remaining reduction.

5. Season to taste, then add the pieces of duck. Simmer until cooked through, about 5 minutes, and serve on shallow plates as described above.

CHAPTER 12

MERLOT

While Merlot is the major grape of Bordeaux's St. Emilion and Pomerol regions—in fact, the entire right bank of the Gironde—it is also the most widely planted variety throughout Bordeaux. Merlot is also grown extensively in southwest France and in the Midi. It is also widely cultivated in northeastern Italy. Usually it is blended with Cabernet Sauvignon to fill in the middle palate of that austere variety and make it taste less tannic. Merlot ripens earlier and matures faster than Cabernet and thus can be consumed with pleasure at a younger age. Merlot berries are larger than those of Cabernet Sauvignon, which means less tannin in the finished wine.

In California, Merlot is now as popular as Cabernet Sauvignon, where it is blended with Cabernet Sauvignon and Cabernet Franc in Bordelais proportions to produce Meritage reds. It is also enjoying a vogue on its own as a varietal wine and commanding Cabernet Sauvignon prices. Some of the finest New World Merlots are coming out of Washington State.

TASTE PROFILE

Merlot has a distinctive plum and blueberry taste, although its structure is similar to Cabernet Sauvignon. It tends to be less tannic and acidic than Cabernet. In warm growing regions where Cabernet ripens well, the distinction is less marked than in Bordeaux.

SYNONYMS

Petit Merle, Vitraille, Crabutet Noir, Bigney

BEST EXPRESSION

Château Pétrus, the greatest Pomerol, generally the better wines of St. Emilion and Pomerol; some Friuli Merlots, Napa Valley and Sonoma Merlots (Newton, Arrowood); Washington—Leonetti, Woodward Canyon, Andrew Will

SUBSTITUTES

Cabernet Sauvignon, Cabernet Franc, Malbec

ROASTED BLACK PEPPERCORN PRIME RIB WITH ROSEMARY AND GARLIC

Serves 8 to 10

If you choose to grill the beef rather than roast it, you may want to consider teaming it with a Cabernet Sauvignon. Roasting the meat softens the flavours somewhat—even with the peppercorn/garlic influence—making the gentler, more elegant Merlot a lovely choice. Reserve this magnificent dish for a special occasion.

8 lb	prime rib roast	4 kg
1 tbsp	black peppercorns	15 mL
1 tbsp	dried rosemary	15 mL
1 tbsp	coarse salt	15 mL
1 tbsp	paprika	15 mL
1 tbsp	hot English mustard	15 mL
4 cloves	garlic, halved	4 cloves
4 sprigs	fresh rosemary	4 sprigs

1. Preheat oven to 425°F (220°C). Trim the roast of excess fat, if necessary. Combine the peppercorns, rosemary, salt and paprika in a coffee or spice grinder and grind to a powder.
2. In a small bowl, blend the ground spices with the mustard thoroughly.
3. Smear the spice-mustard mixture over the entire roast. Using a sharp knife, cut slits, 2 inches (5 cm) apart, into the roast. Insert the garlic and fresh rosemary into alternating slits.
4. Place the beef in a roasting pan, fat side up. Roast for 30 minutes. Cover with foil and continue to roast until beef is cooked to your liking (for a medium-cooked roast, about 18 minutes per pound/500 g, plus an additional 20 minutes).
5. When roasted, remove the foil, turn off the oven and tilt open the oven door. Leave the roast undisturbed for about 30 minutes before carving.

BEEF TOURNEDOS WITH MUSTARD AND ONION SAUCE

Serves 4

Tournedos is a beef steak cut from the tenderloin. Since it is so lean, it is often wrapped with bacon before grilling or pan-frying. In this recipe, the extra flavour boost comes from sautéed onion and garlic, bolstered by mustard and beef broth.

⅓ cup	balsamic vinegar	75 mL
⅓ cup	honey mustard	75 mL
1 lb	beef tenderloin steaks	500 g
1 tsp	coarsely ground black pepper	5 mL
2 tbsp	olive oil	25 mL
1	large onion, thinly sliced	1
2 cloves	garlic, minced	2 cloves
½ cup	beef broth	125 mL
1 tsp	chopped fresh rosemary	5 mL

1. Preheat oven broiler or grill. Combine 1 tbsp (15 mL) each of the balsamic vinegar and honey mustard and brush half on one side of the steaks. Sprinkle steaks with half of the pepper and broil or grill for 3 to 4 minutes. Turn and brush remaining mixture on other side and sprinkle on a little more pepper. Broil for another 3 minutes.

2. In a large skillet, warm the oil over medium heat. Sauté onion and garlic for about 2 minutes. Add remaining vinegar and honey mustard, beef broth and rosemary, and let simmer briskly until onions are cooked through and sauce is slightly thickened, about 5 minutes.

3. To serve, place a steak on each of four plates. Cover with onion sauce and serve with garlic mashed potatoes and crisp-cooked green beans tossed with roasted red pepper strips.

CHEESE, BACON AND POTATO CAKE

Serves 6 to 8

Some potato gratins feature the addition of cream, milk and often eggs to add body and substance to the finished dish. This version relies only on the wonderful quality of Gruyère cheese and the goodness of the hefty potatoes themselves for its success. Of course, good-quality bacon doesn't hurt either. This dish needs nothing more than a big green salad to make it a meal.

2-½ lbs	Yukon Gold potatoes	1.25 kg
1 tbsp	extra virgin olive oil	15 mL
½ lb	good-quality bacon, thinly sliced	125 g
1-½ cups	freshly grated Gruyère cheese	375 mL
	freshly ground black pepper	

1. Peel the potatoes and place them in cold water for 15 minutes or so. Pat them dry and slice thinly; place slices in fresh cold water for another 5 minutes. Pat them thoroughly dry.
2. Preheat oven to 425°F (220°C). Oil the bottom and sides of an oval or round (9-inch/23-cm) baking dish. Arrange the slices of bacon on the bottom and sides of the dish, in a spiral fashion, allowing a little more than half the length of each slice to hang over the side.
3. Use one third of the potato slices to cover the bacon in the dish and sprinkle with one third of the cheese. Repeat this procedure with remaining potatoes and cheese. Use the overhanging bacon to cover the tops of the potatoes. (The potatoes should be exposed in the centre.)
4. Bake dish for about 55 minutes, until bacon is cooked and potatoes are tender and golden.
5. Remove from the oven and let sit for 15 minutes before seasoning with pepper and serving.

CALF'S LIVER WITH CARAMELIZED ONIONS

Serves 4

What is it about the combination of liver and onions that is so good? When you make this version, you'll wonder no more—especially if you team it with a Merlot from California or Washington.

4 pieces	calf's liver, about 6 oz (185 g) each	4 pieces
4 tbsp	olive oil	50 mL
3 tbsp	butter	45 mL
3	large onions, thinly sliced	3
3 tbsp	chopped fresh parsley	45 mL
	salt and freshly ground black pepper	
½–1 cup	Merlot	125–250 mL

1. Cut each piece of liver into three or four pieces. Set aside.
2. In a skillet, heat half the oil and half the butter over medium heat. Add the onions and some of the parsley, a little salt and pepper; stir to blend well. Reduce heat slightly and cook onions slowly for about 20 minutes, loosely covered, stirring occasionally. Then, increase the heat and continue cooking for another 10 minutes or so. Transfer onions to a bowl and keep covered and warm.
3. Heat remaining oil and butter in the same skillet over high heat. Sauté liver for a minute or two, until it is pink (unless you prefer it well done). Transfer liver to a warm serving platter and keep warm.
4. Splash the Merlot and a little more salt and pepper into the skillet. Bring the wine to a boil, scraping up any bits in the pan. Cook a few minutes, until slightly thickened.
5. To serve, scatter the onions over the liver on the serving platter, pour wine reduction over top and sprinkle on remaining parsley. Serve immediately.

CHAPTER 13

NEBBIOLO

What Pinot Noir is to Burgundy, Nebbiolo is to the Piedmont region of northeastern Italy. It is arguably that country's noblest red wine (moreso than the blended Chiantis), even if it is its most austere wine. The grape itself has an ancient lineage and has been documented back to the 13th century. Wines made from the Nebbiolo grape are certainly the longest lived, comparable to red Bordeaux; because of the high tannins and concentration of acids they are rarely approachable until thcy have been tamed by several years in a bottle. Unlike Cabernet Sauvignon and Pinot Noir, Nebbiolo has never really achieved any distinction outside its native Piedmont and even beyond the boundaries of the Barolo and Barbaresco zones, although on occasion Gattinara and Ghemme may rise to the top. It is truly a unique Italian variety that does not travel.

Nebbiolo is a diminutive from the Italian word *nebbia,* meaning fog, which speaks to the climatic condition that happens in the hills around Alba around harvest time.

TASTE PROFILE

Acidic and tannic in its youth, Nebbiolo softens with age, developing a rich and complex bouquet of dried fruits, leather, black cherries, truffles, roses, herbs and tar. It does not have the ready accessibility of Cabernet Sauvignon and exhibits a characteristic bitterness on the finish. There are two winemaking schools—the traditional method of long aging in oak and the contemporary school that bottles the wine earlier to preserve the fruit.

SYNONYMS

Spanna, Chiavennasca, Picotener, Pugnet. (You will find Nebbiolo as a consituent of Lessona, Bramaterra, Boca, Sizzano and Fara and, from Lombardy, Sassella, Grumello, Valgella, Inferno, Valtellina Rosso and Sfursat.)

BEST EXPRESSION

the wines of Barolo (the king of Italian reds) and Barbaresco (more approachable)

SUBSTITUTES

old Rhône reds, mature Sangiovese-based wines (Chianti Riservas)

HUNTER'S RABBIT

Serves 6

Chicken done in this fashion is quite well known outside of Italy as chicken cacciatora. This version, based on rabbit, has loads more flavour and character. There is nothing sophisticated or modern about it—which is precisely what makes it so good. And, like most meat braises, stews and casseroles, it tastes even better the next day. Ask the butcher to section the rabbit if you are bunny-phobic.

4 lb	farm-raised rabbit, sectioned into 10–12 pieces	2 kg
6 cloves	garlic	6 cloves
4 tbsp	fresh rosemary leaves	60 mL
⅓ cup	olive oil	75 mL
½ tsp	salt	2 mL
½ tsp	freshly ground black pepper	2 mL
2 cups	Nebbiolo	500 mL
1 tbsp	tomato paste	15 mL
1-¼ cups	water	300 mL

1. Rinse and pat dry the pieces of rabbit. Slice four of the garlic cloves into slivers. With a small paring knife, make a series of slits in the rabbit and insert the slivers of garlic and most of the rosemary. Chop the remaining garlic cloves with the rest of the rosemary.
2. In a Dutch oven or similar heavy-based pot, heat the oil over medium-high heat and sauté the garlic and rosemary for a minute or two. Add rabbit to the pan, in batches if necessary, and brown all over. Sprinkle with salt and pepper.
3. Splash in the wine and scrape up any bits clinging to the bottom and sides of the pan. Stir in tomato paste and water . Bring to the boil, reduce heat and simmer, uncovered, for about an hour, until rabbit is tender and sauce has thickened. Serve with creamy polenta and lots of good bread.

BEEF TENDERLOIN WITH POT AU FEU OF WINTER VEGETABLES AND BLACK PEPPER AND BREADCRUMB SAUCE AVALON

Serves 6

The chef and owner of Toronto's splendid Avalon, Chris McDonald, has put this truly outstanding recipe together and suggests it would work best with a younger, fruitier Nebbiolo, as in Nebbiolo Galva, rather than a Barolo or Barbaresco. "This sauce is actually a Veronese sauce called *pearà*," he says, "so you might want to match it with a wine from that region, though I do feel it is better matched with the Nebbiolo than an Amarone."

You need a serious quantity of marrow bones for this recipe. Order them from your butcher a day or so in advance. Plan to make the sauce and consommé ahead of time. If the prospect of making your own consommé is too daunting (although, if you have time, you should attempt it), purchase a quantity from a reputable food shop, where it is often sold frozen.

For the Black Pepper and Breadcrumb Sauce

¼ lb	beef or veal bone marrow (about 3 lbs/1.5 kg beef or veal marrow bones)	125 g
¼ lb	butter	125 g
1 cup	dry breadcrumbs	250 mL
2-½ cups	beef or veal broth	625 mL
1-½ tbsp	freshly ground black pepper	22 mL
	salt	

For the consommé

1 lb	very lean stewing beef, cut into small cubes	500 g
1 stalk	celery	1 stalk
1 cup	canned tomatoes	250 mL
1	leek	1
1	medium carrot	1
1	medium onion	1
1	bay leaf	1

1 sprig	fresh thyme	1 sprig
6	egg whites	6
12 cups	cold beef or veal stock	3 L

For the beef

2 lb	beef tenderloin (1 piece)	1 kg
	olive oil for rubbing	
	salt and freshly ground black pepper	
4 cups	beef or veal stock, salted and chilled	1 L
6	carrots, peeled, cut into chunks	6
6	parsnips, peeled, cut into chunks	6
18	Brussels sprouts, trimmed	18
3	large Yukon Gold potatoes, peeled, quartered	3
10 cups	consommé (recipe follows)	2.5 L

1. To make the Black Pepper and Breadcrumb Sauce, extract the raw bone marrow from the bones by loosening the marrow from the bones with a small knife and prizing it out in one piece. (Raw marrow can be wrapped and stored in the refrigerator for 2 to 3 days or in a freezer for up to 2 months.) In a food processor, combine the butter and marrow, and process until the marrow is softened and broken down.

2. In a heavy saucepan, over low heat, melt the mixture down; strain it to remove bone particles and return the mixture to the pan. Stir in bread-crumbs and cook over low heat for 15 minutes. Stir in broth, pepper and salt. Cook for 30 minutes over low heat, stirring occasionally. Set sauce aside.

3. To make the consommé, in a meat grinder with a coarse disk, grind the beef along with all the vegetables and the bay leaf and fresh thyme.

4. In a heavy stock pot, combine this mixture with the egg whites. Stir in the cold stock and bring to a boil over medium-high heat, stirring frequently. When the mixture approaches a boil, stop stirring and allow a "raft" (a thick skin) to form on the surface. Simmer the stock gently for 1 hour.

5. Strain the consommé through a sieve lined with cheesecloth, taking care not to disturb the raft. Reserve the liquid until ready to serve with beef.

6. To make the beef, preheat oven to 450°F (230°C). Rub the beef with oil, salt and pepper. In a cast-iron skillet, sear the beef on all sides over high heat.

Then, roast the beef in the hot oven for 15 minutes (beef should be rare for this dish). Set meat aside in a warm spot to rest.

7. Meanwhile, bring the stock to a simmer in a large pot. Cook the vegetables, individually, in the stock until they are tender; use a slotted spoon to remove them and set them aside in a warm spot. Reheat consommé over medium heat and keep hot.

8. To serve, place equal amounts of vegetables in six large preheated bowls. Slice beef in ½-inch (1-cm) slices and arrange them on top of the vegetables. Ladle about ¾ cup (175 mL) of consommé into each bowl. Serve at once with the Black Pepper and Breadcrumb Sauce at the table.

TORTA RUSTICA

Serves 8

A cross between lasagne and a quiche, this hearty combination of pasta, egg and sausage is lovely served warm with a simple tomato sauce. Look for fresh lasagne pasta for this recipe. You can also cook dry lasagne pasta but you will need double the quantity.

3–4	lean Italian sausages, hot or sweet (to equal about ½ lb/250 g), oven-roasted for 15 minutes, drained	3–4
1	onion, finely chopped	1
½ lb	prosciutto, finely chopped	250 g
1 cup	grated Italian fontina cheese	250 mL
½ cup	grated Parmigiano Reggiano	125 mL
6	eggs, lightly whisked	6
½ cup	light cream	125 mL
½ lb	Swiss chard or spinach, washed, cut into thin strips	250 g
8	sun-dried tomatoes, packed in oil, drained, chopped	8
2 tbsp	chopped flat-leaf parsley	25 mL
	freshly ground black pepper	
8 sheets	fresh pasta (9 x 6 inches/23 x 15 cm), cooked, drained, dried	8 sheets

1. Thinly slice the cooked sausage and combine in a mixing bowl with the onion, prosciutto, two cheeses, eggs, cream, Swiss chard or spinach, and sun-dried tomatoes. Mix together well. Add chopped parsley and black pepper.

2. Preheat oven to 350°F (180°C). Butter the bottom and sides of a 9-inch (23-cm) springform pan. Lay one of the lasagne strips in the centre of the pan and allow it to hang over the edge slightly. Repeat with three more sheets of pasta, overlapping them slightly, until the interior of the pan is completely covered with pasta.

3. Pour half of the sausage and egg mixture into the pan and fold the pasta that is hanging over the edges of the pan to cover the filling. Add the remaining filling and then arrange the remaining sheets of pasta over the top.

4. Bake for 50 to 55 minutes until it is slightly golden brown and a tester inserted in the centre comes out clean.

5. Remove pan from the oven and let it cool for half an hour. Invert pie onto a serving plate and remove the springform pan. Cut pie into wedges and serve as is or with a fresh tomato sauce.

OSSO BUCO ALLA MILANESE

Serves 6

Some versions of osso buco, the renowned Italian stew featuring slow-cooked sections of veal shank, omit the tomato and base the sauce on white wine and chicken broth. In this northern Italian version, however, tomatoes and Nebbiolo make the dish what it is—superb. Serve it with soft polenta or a simple risotto. The *gremolata* (a mixture of finely chopped parsley, garlic and lemon zest), which is added just before serving, elevates the whole dish tremendously.

6	10-oz (300-g) veal shanks	6
¼ cup	seasoned flour for dusting	50 mL
2 tbsp	unsalted butter	25 mL
¼ cup	olive oil	50 mL
2	onions, chopped	2
1-¼ cups	Nebbiolo	300 mL
1-½ cups	canned plum tomatoes, finely chopped	375 mL
1 cup	beef broth	250 mL
½ tsp	salt	2 mL
¼ tsp	freshly ground black pepper	1 mL

For the gremolata

	Finely grated zest of 1 lemon	
⅓ cup	chopped flat-leaf parsley	75 mL
2 cloves	garlic, minced	2 cloves

1. Combine the ingredients for the gremolata and mix well.

2. Dust the veal shanks lightly with the seasoned flour, shaking off the excess. In a large Dutch oven or heavy casserole, melt the butter and add oil over medium-high heat. Brown the veal shanks, a few at a time, until they are nicely browned on all sides. Once they are browned, transfer to a plate.

3. Add onions to the pan and cook until they are softened, about 5 minutes. Add wine to the pan and bring to a gentle boil, scraping up any bits clinging to the bottom and sides of the pan. Gently boil for about 3 minutes.

4. Stir in tomatoes and beef broth. Return the veal shanks to the pan, turning them over once or twice. Add salt and pepper, bring liquid to a gentle boil; reduce heat, cover and let cook gently for 1-½ to 2 hours, or until veal is tender and sauce is nicely thickened. Check the meat every now and then, turning it over occasionally and adding a little water or additional wine, if necessary.

5. Once the sauce is nicely thickened and the veal shanks thoroughly cooked, adjust the seasoning once more. Sprinkle the gremolata over the osso buco just before serving.

CHAPTER 14

SANGIOVESE

Literally translated as the "blood of Jove," Sangiovese is the Cabernet Sauvignon of Italy, responsible for the wines of Chianti, Brunello di Montalcino and Vino Nobile di Montepulciano in Tuscany and planted extensively in other central and southern Italian provinces. It is, in fact, Italy's most widely planted red grape. Although Sangiovese is generally blended with other red wines (particularly with Canaiolo in Chianti), it can make fine varietal wine on its own, as it does in Brunello as well as in some California vineyards. It reaches its peak of perfection when blended with up to 20 per cent Cabernet Sauvignon, the recipe for many of the "Super Tuscan" blends.

Since Chianti was granted the appellation DOCG, the wines have improved enormously. The virtual eradication of white wines from the blend in favour of Cabernet Sauvignon, Merlot or Syrah has given the wine a new distinction.

TASTE PROFILE

A firm wine, medium-bodied, dry, with a bouquet of chestnut with a floral note and a bitter finish. Flavours of cherries, plums, currants, but always with a healthy spine of acidity that matches well with tomato-based dishes. Tends to brown with age, taking on leather, barnyard and truffle notes.

SYNONYMS

Brunello, Morellino, Nielluccio (Corsica), Prugnolo, Sangioveto

BEST EXPRESSION

pure Sangiovese—Brunello di Montalcino, La Pregole Torte di Monte Vertine, Badia a Coltibuono; blended—Chianti Classico Riservas, Vino Nobile di Montepulciano, Super Tuscan wines, Rubesco Riserva (Umbria)

SUBSTITUTES

Barbera, Vapolicella

OYSTER JIM'S CLAYOQUOT ROASTING OYSTERS WITH TOMATO COMPÔTE AND PARMESAN CRUST

Makes 12 appetizers

From Chef Rodney Butters at The Pointe Restaurant at Canada's Wickaninnish Inn. Use large Pacific oysters for this dish.

1 tsp	pure olive oil	5 mL
1	small white onion, chopped	1
½ bulb	fennel, chopped	½ bulb
2	tomatoes, peeled, seeded, chopped (fresh or canned)	2
1 tbsp	fresh chopped thyme	15 mL
3 slices	day-old white bread	3 slices
2 tbsp	fresh chopped flat-leaf parsley	25 mL
3 oz	Parmigiano Reggiano, grated	90 g
12	large fresh shucked oysters	12

1. Preheat oven to 425°F (220°C). In a skillet over medium heat, warm the oil and sauté onion and fennel for a minute. Add the tomato and thyme and cook for 5 minutes.

2. Meanwhile, trim crusts from the bread and process to a fine crumb in a food processor. In a mixing bowl, combine breadcrumbs with chopped parsley and grated cheese.

3. Spoon tomato mixture over top of each oyster, followed by a topping of breadcrumb mixture, patting it lightly into place. Bake in preheated oven for 5 to 8 minutes. Serve immediately.

POLPETTE DI CARNE

Serves 6

If you make these delicious little meatballs large and serve them with pasta or rice, they make a nice main course for four. They're versatile, too—you can serve them in tomato sauce for a Sicilian twist, or you can serve them on their own as an appetizer.

1 lb	lean ground beef	500 g
1 lb	lean ground pork	500 g
¾ cup	dry breadcrumbs	175 mL
¾ cup	grated Pecorino Romano	175 mL
1	large egg	1
	salt and freshly ground black pepper	
3 tbsp	chopped flat-leaf parsley	45 mL
	zest of 1 large lemon, finely grated, and its juice	
2 cloves	garlic, finely chopped	2 cloves
⅓ cup	golden raisins, chopped	75 mL
¼ tsp	freshly grated nutmeg	1 mL
⅓ cup	pine nuts	75 mL
½ cup (approx.)	all-purpose flour	125 mL (approx.)
⅓ cup	pure olive oil (for frying)	75 mL
4–5 cups	tomato sauce, preferably homemade (optional)	1–1.25 L

1. Combine in a large mixing bowl the beef, pork, breadcrumbs, cheese, egg, salt, pepper, parsley, lemon zest, lemon juice, garlic, raisins, nutmeg and pine nuts, and mix to combine thoroughly.

2. Shape into little balls. If you plan to fry the meatballs, roll them in the flour, shaking off excess. Warm oil in a large skillet and fry, shaking the pan from time to time to help meatballs roll around and retain their shape, for about 25 minutes or until they are cooked through.

3. Alternatively, heat the tomato sauce in a large Dutch oven, add the shaped meatballs to the sauce and cook for about an hour or so. Serve with lots of good bread.

BUCATINI WITH FENNEL AND TOMATO

Serves 6

The Italians often choose to nibble on fresh fennel at the close of a meal to aid digestion. In this simple uncooked sauce, thinly sliced fennel—with its strong anise flavour—and fresh tomato combine to make a light-tasting but flavourful foil for hot pasta. Make this dish when fresh, ripe tomatoes are plentiful. The quality of this sauce improves dramatically if it is allowed to sit at room temperature for at least an hour before serving. It is very nice with grilled fish steaks.

2 heads	fresh fennel, tops removed, bulbs sliced very thinly lengthwise	2 heads
1 lb	fresh ripe plum tomatoes, peeled, seeded, finely chopped	500 g
2 cloves	garlic, finely chopped	2 cloves
¼ cup	extra virgin olive oil	50 mL
	salt and freshly ground black pepper	
¼ cup	chopped flat-leaf parsley	50 mL
	juice of 1 lemon, finely chopped zest of 1 lemon	
1 tsp	coarse salt	5 mL
1 lb	bucatini (or similar pasta)	500 g

1. Trim fennel, remove the tough outer leaves, quarter the bulbs and rinse them clean. Cut them into very thin slices across their width.
2. In a large bowl, combine the fennel and the tomato, garlic, oil, salt, pepper, parsley, lemon juice and zest. Mix well. Allow to sit at room temperature, covered, for 2 hours. (Or prepare the night before, cover and refrigerate. Allow to return to room temperature before serving.)
3. Bring a large pot of water to boil, add coarse salt and cook pasta until it is tender but firm. Drain, add it to the fennel-tomato mixture and toss lightly. Serve immediately.

PENNE WITH WILD MUSHROOMS AND TOMATOES

Serves 6

Use any assortment of mushrooms you prefer, but try to include some "wild" varieties and perhaps some dry and rehydrated porcini. Penne rigate is the quill-shaped pasta with the little grooves or ridges.

3 tbsp	pure olive oil	45 mL
2 cloves	garlic, finely chopped	2 cloves
2	medium-sized onions, chopped	2
1 tbsp	butter	15 mL
2 cups	sliced assorted mushrooms	500 mL
1 cup	finely chopped Italian plum tomatoes, fresh or canned	250 mL
1 tsp	coarse salt	5 mL
1 lb	penne rigate	500 g
½ cup	light cream	125 mL
	salt and freshly ground black pepper	
2 tbsp	chopped flat-leaf parsley	25 mL
1 cup	grated Parmigiano Reggiano	250 mL

1. Place a large pot of water on to boil. In a large skillet, warm oil over moderate heat. Add garlic and onion and sauté until they are softened, about 3 minutes. Add butter and mushrooms and cook for a further 3 minutes.

2. Add tomatoes, mix together well, and cook until slightly thickened, about 10 to 12 minutes. Add coase salt and pasta to boiling water, stir once and cook until pasta is tender but firm.

3. Add cream, salt and pepper and parsley, and gently boil for 3 minutes. When pasta is cooked, drain well and add to sauce. Mix together over low heat and add grated Parmigiano Reggiano. Toss together gently and serve immediately.

EGGPLANT PARMIGIANA

Serves 6

There is nothing quite as satisfying as an honest-to-goodness eggplant parmigiana. As good at room temperature as it is hot, this dish also makes a wonderful filling for crusty bread rolls or as an accompaniment to scrambled eggs for brunch.

3–4	medium-sized eggplant, sliced ¼-inch (6-mm) thick	3–4
	salt as needed	
2 cups	dry breadcrumbs	500 mL
2	large eggs	2
	vegetable oil for frying as needed	
4 cups	quality tomato sauce	1 L
1-½ cups	grated Parmigiano Reggiano	375 mL
3 cups	shredded mozzarella	750 mL

1. Lay the slices of eggplant on paper towels and sprinkle them lightly on both sides with salt. Leave for 20 minutes or so to drain. Pat slices dry.
2. Scatter breadcrumbs in a shallow dish. In another shallow dish, beat eggs with a little salt until they are foamy. Dip eggplant slices in egg, then dip in breadcrumbs to coat both sides, patting the crumbs firmly in place on the eggplant. Repeat until all eggplant slices are coated.
3. Heat oil in a large skillet over medium heat. Fry eggplant slices, a few at a time, on both sides until golden brown. Transfer them to paper towels to drain. When all the slices have been cooked, cover with fresh paper towels to absorb any remaining oil. Leave for 20 minutes. Preheat oven to 400°F (200°C).
4. In an 11- x 13-inch (28- x 33-cm) baking dish, ladle out enough tomato sauce to cover the bottom. Add a layer of eggplant and sprinkle it with ½ cup (125 mL) of the Parmigiano Reggiano and 1 cup (250 mL) of the mozzarella. Add a second layer of eggplant, cover with tomato sauce and layer with the two cheeses once again. Repeat for two more layers, ending with remaining sauce.
5. Cover with foil and bake in preheated oven for about an hour. Let stand for 20 minutes before serving.

ROAST TOMATOES GRATIN

Serves 6 to 8

Serve these fat, luscious tomatoes alongside hot pasta tossed with nothing more than excellent olive oil and lots of freshly grated Parmigiano Reggiano. They are very good as an accompaniment to hefty grilled sausages, roast chicken or beef. Choose vine-ripened beefsteak tomatoes if available.

¼ cup	extra virgin olive oil	50 mL
8	large ripe, firm tomatoes, halved across the width	8
	salt and freshly ground black pepper	
¼ cup	chopped flat-leaf parsley	50 mL
2 tsp	chopped fresh oregano	10 mL
4 cloves	garlic, minced	4 cloves
1-½ cups	dry breadcrumbs (depending on size of tomatoes)	375 mL

1. Preheat oven to 400°F (200°C). In a large skillet, heat the oil over medium-high heat. Add tomatoes, cut side down, to the skillet in batches and sear them for about 3 to 4 minutes. Don't move them about.

2. Transfer tomatoes, cooked side up, to a baking dish large enough to accommodate them in one layer.

3. In a mixing bowl, combine the salt, pepper, parsley, oregano, garlic and 1 cup (250 mL) of the breadcrumbs. Toss to mix well. Add the remaining breadcrumbs to the bowl if necessary. Top the tomatoes with this mixture, pressing it into place.

4. Drizzle any accumulated pan juices over tomatoes and bake, uncovered, until the topping is golden brown, about 15 to 20 minutes, watching them to make sure the topping is not browning too quickly. Serve immediately.

CHAPTER 15

TEMPRANILLO

Temperano in Spanish means "early," which refers to the vine's ripening abilities. Tempranillo is the main constituent in some of Spain's longest-lived and most elegant red wines, in spite of its low acidity and low alcohol. Although you do see it today in the Rioja region as a varietal wine, it is usually blended with Garnacha and some Mazuelo and Graciano. This blend recalls the Bordeaux style of winemaking, speaking to the era at the end of the 19th century when phylloxera destroyed the vineyards of France and winemakers crossed the Pyrenees to create vineyards untainted by the blight. It is not much grown outside of Spain, apart from being one of the five recommended grapes for port (as Tinto Roriz) and as a varietal table wine in Argentina.

TASTE PROFILE

A deeply coloured, light- to medium-bodied wine when young, it has a taste of strawberries, raspberries or cherries. It can resemble red Bordeaux when young and Burgundy when aged in bottle for several years. Usually matured in American oak, it takes on an exotic, spice bouquet, which is rather like sandalwood.

SYNONYMS

Ull de Lebre (Penedès), Cencibel (La Mancha), Tinto Fino (Ribera del Duero), Tinto di Toro, Tinta Roriz (Portugal)

BEST EXPRESSION
Rioja, Navarra; Ribera del Duero—Vega Sicilia, Pesquera; Penedès—Coronas

SUBSTITUTES
red Burgundy, Alsace Pinot Noir, German Spätburgunder Spätlese

CHICK PEAS AND SAUSAGE

Serves 4-6

A dish with a Spanish accent, this is guaranteed to ward off the cold. A variation on this dish is made throughout Spain, sometimes with black beans or pinto beans, depending on the area. This one hails from Galicia, in the northwest pocket of the country. It is good hot or at room temperature, as it is or as a filling for a warmed tortilla.

2-½ cups	dried chick peas, soaked overnight	625 mL
1 cup	chicken broth	250 mL
1 cup	tomato juice	250 mL
1-½ cups	water	375 mL
2 tbsp	olive oil	25 mL
1	large onion, chopped	1
½ lb	spicy sausage (chorizo or other)	250 g
½ lb	mild sausage	250 g
2 cloves	garlic, finely chopped	2 cloves
½ cup	roasted red pepper strips	125 mL
1 tbsp	tomato paste	15 mL
1 tsp	paprika	5 mL
	salt and freshly ground black pepper	

1. Drain and rinse chick peas. Place them in a large pot with the chicken broth, tomato juice and water to cover. Add more water if necessary. Bring to a boil over high heat. Reduce heat and simmer for 1 to 1-½ hours, until tender.

2. Meanwhile, in a skillet warm the oil over medium-high heat. Sauté the onion until soft, about 5 minutes. Cut the sausages into chunks and add them to the skillet. Continue to sauté for about 20 minutes, turning the sausage chunks over to brown and cook evenly. Add the garlic halfway through the cooking time.

3. When sausages are cooked and the chick peas tender, scrape the contents of the skillet, including the juices, into the pot containing the chick peas. Stir to combine well.

4. Stir in the strips of red pepper, the tomato paste and the paprika. Simmer for another 10 minutes. Taste for seasoning and serve.

PAELLA

Serves 6 to 8

Curiously, once paella is out of its country of origin, Spain's renowned and extravagant one-dish meal is usually accompanied by a crisp white wine. Not in Spain, however, where Tempranillo-based Riojas are seen as the best partners to everything from wild boar to fish and seafood. Cabernet Sauvignon is also a good choice.

1 lb	raw jumbo shrimp	500 g
3 lb	chicken	1.5 kg
¼ cup	olive oil	50 mL
1	chorizo (spicy Spanish sausage), thickly sliced	1
½ lb	ham, cubed	250 g
1	large red onion, chopped	1
2 cloves	garlic, crushed	2 cloves
2	ripe tomatoes, chopped	2
2 tsp	tomato paste	10 mL
1 cup	dry white wine	250 mL
1 tsp	saffron	5 mL
2-¼ cups	short-grain rice	550 mL
4 cups	chicken stock	1 L
12	clams, in the shell	12
12	mussels, in the shell	12
1	red bell pepper, seeded, sliced	1
1 cup	peas, fresh or frozen	250 mL
1 lb	cooked lobster, cut into chunks	500 g
1 tbsp	capers, drained	15 mL
2 tbsp	chopped fresh parsley	25 mL
1	lemon, cut into wedges	1

1. Peel and devein shrimp, leaving tail intact. Cut the chicken into serving pieces. Remove and discard the back bone and wing tips (or keep for making stock). Trim excess fat and skin.

2. In a large Dutch oven or traditional paella pan, warm oil over medium heat. Add chicken, chorizo and ham, and cook, turning and stirring frequently, until the chicken is golden brown, about 8 to 10 minutes.

3. Using a slotted spoon, transfer the chicken, chorizo and ham to a plate.

4. Add shrimp to the pan and cook, stirring frequently, until shrimp turn pink, no more than 4 minutes. Using a slotted spoon, transfer shrimp to the plate.

5. Preheat oven to 350°F (180°C). If necessary, add a little more oil to the pan. Add onion and garlic to the pan, and cook, stirring occasionally, until onion is soft, about 3 minutes. Reduce heat to low, add tomatoes and tomato paste to the pan, and simmer for 5 minutes.

6. Meanwhile, heat ¼ cup (50 mL) wine in a small saucepan over low heat. Pour wine over saffron in a small bowl. Let soak for a few minutes, strain and add liquid to the pan with the onion and tomato mixture.

7. Add rice, stock and remaining wine to the pan. Bring mixture to a boil, stirring continuously, then remove pan from heat. Arrange the chicken, chorizo, ham, clams, mussels and red pepper slices over the rice. Sprinkle peas over the surface. Cover the pan with a lid or securely with foil.

8. Bake until rice is tender, about 30 minutes. Without disturbing the mixture, place the shrimp, lobster and capers on top and bake, uncovered, for an additional 5 minutes. Sprinkle with parsley and serve with lemon.

BRAISED LAMB SHANKS WITH OVEN-ROASTED PARSNIPS

Serves 6

Comforting and satisfying, these hearty lamb shanks provide as much flavour and taste appeal as any upscale lamb cut. Serve with potatoes mashed with butter, cream and green onions, known as "champ" in Ireland, which is exactly how you'll feel after eating them.

6	lamb shanks	6
3 tbsp	all-purpose flour	45 mL
	salt and freshly ground black pepper	
1 tsp	herbes de Provence	5 mL
⅓ cup + 1 tbsp	olive oil	75 mL + 15 mL
1	large cooking onion, chopped	1
2 stalks	celery, chopped	2 stalks
2	carrots, chopped	2
2 cloves	garlic, finely chopped	2 cloves
	bouquet garni of flat-leaf parsley, rosemary, thyme, celery leaf tied together	
1 cup	dry red wine	250 mL
1 cup	beef stock	250 mL
2 lbs	parsnips	1 kg
	fresh chopped parsley	

1. Preheat oven to 350°F (180°C).

2. Wipe lamb shanks with paper towels. In a plastic bag, combine flour, salt, pepper and herbes de Provence. Place lamb shanks (one at a time if they are very large) in the bag and shake to coat well. Shake off excess flour and set to one side.

3. In a Dutch oven or cast-iron pan, warm ⅓ cup (75 mL) oil. Brown lamb shanks, then transfer to large earthenware casserole or other ovenproof dish with a lid. Add onions, celery, carrots, garlic and bouquet garni to the pan and cook, stirring, for 5 minutes.

4. Add wine and beef stock to the pan and bring to the boil for a few minutes, scraping up any bits on the bottom of the pan.

5. Pour this mixture over the lamb shanks. Cover and place in the oven for 1-½ hours or until meat is tender.

6. Slice pasnips lengthwise into equal-sized strips. Toss them in remaining oil, salt and pepper. Place them in the oven and roast them until they are softened and golden brown, about 45 minutes. Sprinkle lamb and parsnips with parsley and serve with mashed potatoes as described above.

LAMB WITH RED WINE AND ROSEMARY

Serves 4 to 6

A good butcher should be able to supply you with boneless shoulder of lamb, which is the best cut for this recipe. Of course, bone-in shoulder of lamb can be used if you don't mind dealing with the bones. Otherwise, use boneless leg of lamb, but reduce cooking time by half.

¼ cup	pure olive oil	50 mL
1	large onion, thinly sliced	1
3 lbs	boneless shoulder of lamb, trimmed of excess fat, cut into 1-inch (2.5-cm) chunks	1.5 kg
	salt and freshly ground black pepper	
1 cup	Tempranillo	250 mL
3 cloves	garlic, peeled and smashed	3 cloves
4 branches	rosemary	4 branches
½ cup	chopped flat-leaf parsley	125 mL

1. In a Dutch oven or heavy casserole, warm the oil over medium-high heat. Sauté the onion until softened, about 5 minutes. Add lamb and season with salt and pepper.

2. Splash in the wine, add garlic and rosemary, and stir to combine well. Increase the heat slightly and bring to a gentle boil; reduce heat immediately to low, cover and simmer for about 2 hours until lamb is tender. Make sure to cook the lamb slowly over low heat.

3. Adjust seasoning. Add the chopped parsley and serve immediately.

OXTAILS IN TEMPRANILLO

Serves 4

My Basque-born friend, chef Teresa Barrenechea of the renowned Marichu restaurant in Bronxville, New York, says this is the way they cook oxtails in Bilbao. Actually, what Teresa really said was this is how they cook the tails of slain fighting bulls during Bilbao's Semana Grande, an annual week-long festival that includes bull-fighting, street parties and cooking contests. But even Spaniards can't always get their hands on a fresh bull's tail; when they can't, they make this fabulous oxtail stew. This is my variation on Teresa's recipe that appeared in her beautiful tribute to Basque cooking, *The Basque Table* (published by Harvard Common Press). Plan to make this terrifically good dish the day before serving. It only gets better.

4 lbs	oxtails, cut into 2-inch (5-cm) pieces (ask the butcher to do this for you if they don't come precut)	2 kg
	salt and freshly ground black pepper	
3 tbsp	all-purpose flour	45 mL
½ cup	olive oil	125 mL
1	medium onion, chopped	1
2	medium carrots, chopped	2
2	medium tomatoes, diced	2
2	leeks, trimmed, slit and rinsed well under cold water, chopped	2

2 cloves	garlic, chopped	2 cloves
3 cups	Tempranillo or red Rioja	750 mL
2 cups	water	500 mL

1. Trim the oxtails of as much fat as possible. In a large bowl, cover them with cold water and leave to soak for a few hours. Drain and rinse under cold running water, then dry thoroughly with paper towels. Sprinkle the oxtails with salt and pepper. Place flour in a plastic bag, add oxtails and shake them until lightly coated with flour, shaking off the excess.

2. In a Dutch oven or similar heavy pot, heat oil over medium heat. Add the onion, carrots, tomatoes, leeks and garlic, and stir to combine all the ingredients well. Cook, stirring, until vegetables begin to soften, about 6 minutes.

3. Add pieces of oxtail and brown on all sides, turning frequently. Pour in the wine and the water, increase the heat slightly, and cook at a gentle boil for about 3 minutes. Reduce heat and let simmer 4 to 5 hours, checking occasionally to make sure the sauce is not drying out. If so, add more wine.

4. When oxtails are tender, use a slotted spoon to transfer them to a large platter, let cool, then cover with plastic wrap and refrigerate overnight. Strain the sauce through a sieve into a large bowl; discard solids. Cool and cover with plastic wrap to sit in the refrigerator overnight.

5. When ready to serve, remove and discard any fat that has solidified atop the surface of the sauce. Return sauce to the heat along with the oxtails and let simmer until thoroughly heated through.

CHAPTER 16

ZINFANDEL

Like Pinotage in South Africa, Zinfandel is unique to California, although there is some debate as to its ancestry. It is similar in style to the Primitivo grape grown in Apulia at the heel of Italy and for ampelographers the shape and size of the leaves are identical. Ever since the 1880s, Zinfandel became the work-horse grape of the California wine industry, but its popularity eventually became its downfall: in the early 1970s, the American wine-drinking public took to white wine with a vengeance. Farmers with Zinfandel in the ground were forced to either grub up their vines and replant Chardonnay or graft Chardonnay onto their vines. The only factor that spared Zinfandel from becoming forgotten was the creation of white Zinfandel (a blush wine with a touch of sweetness). Now the pendulum has swung back and Zinfandel, in its full lusty glory as a fruity red, is now the signature wine of the Golden State. Old Vine Zins from vineyards dating back three or four generations are now all the rage. Zinfandel is also successfully grown in South Africa and in Western Australia.

TASTE PROFILE

Depending on how it is made into wine, Zinfandel can produce a range of wines, from fruity Beaujolais style to late-harvest port-like wines. Generally, it is produced in the medium- to full-bodied style of dense, highly extracted wines with a blackberry or black cherry flavour and a peppery finish, buttressed by smoky, vanilla oak.

SYNONYMS

Primitivo

BEST EXPRESSION
California—Ridge, Ravenswood, Rosenblum, Cline

SUBSTITUTES
Northern Rhône reds, Syrah, Châteauneuf-du-Pape, Amarone, Montefalco Rosso, Shiraz

SAUSAGE AND RAPINI

Serves 6

Choose a spicy Zinfandel that can stand up to the slight spice heat of the sausages and the bitter quality of the greens in this very traditional pairing.

6	hot, lean Italian sausages	6
1 lb	rapini, washed, trimmed	500 g
3 tbsp	pure olive oil	45 mL
6 cloves	garlic, roughly chopped	6 cloves
1-½ tsp	hot pepper flakes	7 mL
	salt and freshly ground black pepper	

1. Preheat oven to 450°F (230°C). Roast sausages for about 15 minutes. While they are roasting, wash and trim rapini.

2. In a heavy Dutch oven or similar pot, warm the oil and sauté the garlic until softened; do not let it brown. Add rapini, pepper flakes, salt, pepper and a splash of water. Mix to combine well, cover and cook 5 to 7 minutes, stirring now and then.

3. Remove sausages from oven, let them cool slightly so you can handle them. Slice sausages on the diagonal and combine with the rapini. Serve at once.

LAMB STEW WITH OLIVES

Serves 6

A good butcher should be able to provide you with shoulder of lamb—the first choice for this particularly good stew, because it lends special flavour and texture. However, boneless lamb also gives good results. Buy good-quality olives from a delicatessen for this dish. If you prefer, all black or all green can be used. Choose a robust Zinfandel for this dish.

3 lbs	lamb shoulder, cut into 2-inch (5 cm) pieces	1.5 kg
	salt and freshly ground black pepper	
3 tbsp	olive oil	45 mL
3 cloves	garlic, chopped	3 cloves
2	large onions, chopped	2
½ tsp	ground cumin	2 mL
2 tsp	chopped fresh oregano	10 mL
3 cups	chicken broth	750 mL
1-¼ cups	Zinfandel	300 mL
½ cup	golden raisins	125 mL
1 cup	pitted black olives, roughly chopped	250 mL
1 cup	pitted green olives, roughly chopped	250 mL
1 cup	chopped fresh parsley	250 mL

1. Season the lamb with a little salt and pepper. In a Dutch oven or similar heavy pot, heat the oil over high heat. Brown the lamb on all sides, in batches, transferring it to a plate when it is cooked.

2. Sauté the garlic, onions and cumin in the pan for about 10 minutes until they are softened. Add oregano, broth, wine and raisins, and bring to a gentle boil, reduce heat and return the lamb to the pan. Bring mixture to the boil once more, reduce heat and allow stew to simmer, loosely covered, for 1-½ hours, until meat is tender.

3. Half an hour before you wish to serve the stew, add the olives; mix well and continue to simmer the stew. Just before serving, add the chopped parsley. Serve with rice or boiled new potatoes tossed in butter and chives.

GRILLED LONDON BROIL

Serves 6

A London broil is a large flank steak that has been marinated, grilled and sliced across the grain into thin diagonal slices, all of which help to make an otherwise highly resistant piece of beef completely irresistible. Make a simple compound butter to accompany the finished dish, perhaps with a chive, parsley and garlic base.

2 cloves	garlic, minced	2 cloves
2	large shallots, finely chopped	2
1 cup	Zinfandel	250 mL
⅓ cup	olive oil	75 mL
	salt and freshly ground black pepper	
2 lb	flank steak	1 kg

1. In a dish large enough to accommodate the flank steak, combine garlic, shallots, wine, oil, salt and pepper. Mix to combine well, lay the flank steak in the marinade, turning it over once or twice, cover with plastic wrap and refrigerate 8 hours or overnight, turning a few times.

2. Allow the meat to return to room temperature before grilling. Preheat grill to medium-high. Remove beef from the marinade and grill, turning once or twice, for about 10 to 15 minutes in total for medium cooked steak. Brush the reserved marinade onto the beef as it cooks.

3. Transfer grilled steak to a cutting board. Allow it to rest for a minute or two before slicing thinly on diagonal across grain. Serve with grilled mixed vegetables.

BARBECUED DUCK PASTA

Serves 6

Duck and pasta are rarely combined, but the results—especially when with a Chinese barbecued duck—are outstanding. The art of duck barbecuing has been perfected by the Chinese, so, rather than go through the years of training involved, pick one up from a reputable Chinese restaurant or barbecue meat shop on your way home. Dinner is almost ready!

5 lb	Chinese barbecued duck	2.25 kg
¼ cup	olive oil	50 mL
1	large red onion, thinly sliced	1
2	red bell peppers, seeded, cut into thin strips	2
½ lb	mushrooms, wiped clean, quartered	250 g
3 cups	chicken broth	750 mL
3 cloves	garlic, minced	3 cloves
3	small zucchini, thinly sliced	3
2	small carrots, cut into thin strips	2
½ lb	thin green beans, trimmed, cut into 2-inch (5-cm) lengths	250 g
1 cup	fresh basil leaves, stacked, cut into thin strips	250 mL
1-½ lbs	fettuccine, cooked as per package instructions	750 g

1. Remove all the meat from the duck, discarding bones, fat and skin (or reserve them for making stock). Cut the meat into strips and set aside.
2. In a large skillet or wok, heat the oil over high heat. Toss in red onion, red peppers and mushrooms, and stir-fry for 2 to 3 minutes. Add chicken broth and garlic, and bring to a lively boil. Boil for 3 minutes to reduce liquid.
3. Add zucchini, carrots, green beans and duck meat; reduce heat and simmer for 2 to 3 minutes more. Add basil, toss together for ½ minute, then serve over the cooked pasta.

PROSCIUTTO PIZZA BIANCA

Serves 4

Make your own pizza dough, if you have a reliable recipe and the time, or pick up a ball of dough from a bakery, supermarket freezer or pizza outlet. This dish makes a lovely appetizer for four or a meal for two with a mixed green salad. Buy the best prosciutto to make this the best pizza you've ever had.

1	uncooked pizza crust	1
2 cloves	garlic, peeled, halved	2 cloves
1 tbsp	dried red chile pepper, crushed fine (or less, to your taste)	15 mL
¼ cup	extra virgin olive oil	50 mL
¾ lb	smoked mozzarella, shredded	175 mL
¼ lb	Italian fontina, shredded	125 g
1 cup	roasted red pepper strips	250 mL
½ cup	roughly chopped fresh basil leaves	125 mL
½ lb	Italian prosciutto, cut into thin strips	250 g
1	red onion, thinly sliced	1
¼ lb	mild goat cheese, crumbled	125 g

1. Preheat oven to 500°F (260°C). Rub the pizza crust with the garlic. Add the chile pepper to the oil and brush it over the surface of the dough.
2. In a mixing bowl, combine the mozzarella and fontina cheese. Toss them together to blend well. Sprinkle all but 1 cup (250 mL) of the cheese over the pizza dough. Add red peppers, basil, prosciutto and red onion. Sprinkle the goat cheese over all and end with the remaining grated cheeses.
3. Bake in a preheated oven for 15 minutes, until crust is golden brown and cheese is bubbling. Serve immediately.

SOUTHBROOK FARM'S CHOCOLATE
BREAD PUDDING

Serves 8

Go ahead—be adventurous, amaze your friends and yourself, and team this outstanding dessert from Ontario's Southbrook Farms with a Late-Harvest Zinfandel.

9 slices	egg bread (challah)	9 slices
5 oz	dark chocolate	155 g
2 cups	light cream	500 mL
½ cup	Southbrook Farm's Framboise	125 mL
½ cup	sugar	125 mL
3 oz	butter	75 g
3	eggs	3

1. Set a large pot of water on to boil. Trim crusts from the bread and cut each slice into four triangles.
2. In a bowl, combine chocolate, cream, Framboise, sugar and butter, and set the bowl over but not touching the hot water. Once the chocolate has melted, whisk it lightly. Remove it from heat and let it cool slightly for a minute or two.
3. In another bowl, whisk the eggs together. Whisk a bit of the chocolate mixture into the eggs. When it is well incorporated, whisk in the remaining chocolate mixture.
4. Lightly grease a 7- x 9-inch (18- x 23-cm) pan. Pour half the chocolate mixture on the bottom of the pan. Cover it with one third of the bread. Repeat, finishing with the chocolate mixture. Press down on the covered bread with a fork to help the chocolate mixture soak in.
5. Cover with plastic wrap and let sit, unrefrigerated, for 2 hours. Place in the refrigerator for 24 to 48 hours.
6. Preheat oven to 350°F (180°C). Bake bread pudding for 30 to 35 minutes. Remove it from the oven and let stand for 5 minutes. Serve with a little Framboise poured over top.

CHAPTER 17
FORTIFIED WINES

SHERRY

The sherry region of Spain is in the bottom left-hand corner of that country, a hot region where the Palomino grape is grown. The wine from this grape is blended with Muscat of Alexandria and Pedro Ximénez (PX) for the sweeter styles of sherry. It can range from delicately bone dry and pale (Fino and Manzanilla) to the heavy, mahogany-coloured sweetness of Cream Sherry.

Sherry is fortified with brandy to bring it up to a minimum level of alcohol of 15.5 per cent. Generally speaking, the deeper the colour, the higher the alcohol, which can rise to a permitted maximum of 20.9 per cent.

Sherry is, without doubt, the most food-friendly of fortified wines. George Saintsbury, an Oxford professor and the author of the 1920 classic work *Notes on a Cellarbook,* suggested a meal in which sherry was served throughout: "Manzanilla with oysters; Montilla with soup and fish; an Amontillado with entrées and roast; an Amoroso or some such with sweets and for after dinner, the oldest and brownest of 'old Brown' …"

Fino and Manzanilla (a wine from the coastal region with a tangy saltiness) can be used as aperitif wines to stimulate appetite or as an accompaniment for fish and seafood. The flavour is of camomile with a spicy bitterness. Best served chilled.

Amontillado is an aged Fino. It is deeper in colour and higher in alcohol, and has a dry nutty taste. Chill lightly. Good with soups—either in the bowl or in the glass.

Oloroso (meaning "fragrant") is a full-bodied nutty wine that can be dry or sweet as labelled. It can stand up to meat dishes and highly spiced foods.

Pale Cream, as the name suggests, is light in colour but sweet. Match it with cake or fruit-based desserts. *Cream* is dark, rich and heavy, with a dried raisin and nut flavour. It can stand up to Christmas pudding.

BEST EXPRESSION

Lustau sherries

SUBSTITUTES

Madeira (Sercial, Verdelho, Bual, Malmsey), white Port, Vin Santo

CHICKEN LIVERS WITH SHERRY AND SHALLOTS ON CROSTINI

Serves 4

If you can find them easily (and like a bit of extra richness), use duck livers for this first course.

3 tbsp	pure olive oil	45 mL
12 oz	fresh, cleaned chicken or duck livers	300 g
4 tbsp	dry sherry	50 mL
2	shallots, finely chopped	2
4 tbsp	unsalted butter	50 mL
	salt and freshly ground black pepper	
12 slices	baguette	12 slices
1 large clove	garlic, halved	1 large clove
2 tbsp	chopped flat-leaf parsley	25 mL

1. In a skillet large enough to hold all the livers without crowding, warm the oil over medium heat. Sauté the livers in the skillet and cook until they are still pink in the centre. Don't let the exterior of the livers get crusty; they should remain soft.

2. With a slotted spoon, remove livers from the pan and pour the sherry into the pan to deglaze. Turn heat down and add shallots to the pan with the sherry. Cook the shallots until softened, about 5 minutes. Remove them from heat and let them cool.

3. Transfer the contents of the pan, the livers and the butter to the bowl of a food processor and purée together until they are smooth; do not over-process. Add salt and pepper as necessary.

4. Toast baguette slices and rub them with cut half of garlic. Spread liver mixture on each slice and sprinkle with a little parsley. Serve immediately.

AJO BLANCO BARRENECHEA

Serves 4 to 6

My friend Teresa Barrenechea is the chef and owner of the widely acclaimed Marichu Restaurant in New York, which, according to the Spanish National Board of Tourism, serves the most authentic Spanish food in the U.S. I travelled with Teresa in her beautiful native country, where I first tasted this incredibly good cold almond soup accompanied by chilled Manzanilla. When I returned home to work on this book, I asked Teresa for a recipe and here it is. Very Spanish and wickedly good—just like Teresa! Choosing authentic Spanish sherry vinegar is important to the success of the finished dish. This soup is wonderfully refreshing on a hot summer day.

1	crusty white bread roll, halved	1
1-½ cups	blanched sliced almonds	375 mL
2 cloves	garlic, peeled	2 cloves
¼ cup	sherry vinegar	50 mL
½ cup	extra virgin olive oil	125 mL
½ tsp	salt	2 mL
4 cups	cold water	1 L
	peeled, seedless green grapes	
	sliced almonds	

1. In a small bowl, soak the bread roll in water for 15 minutes or so. Using your hands, squeeze excess water from the bread. Set bread aside.
2. In a food processor, combine the almonds and garlic, and process until almonds are finely ground. Add bread, vinegar, oil, salt and water, and process the mixture until a smooth texture is formed, about 2 minutes or so.
3. Pour soup into a bowl, cover with plastic wrap and refrigerate until it is quite cold. To serve, pour into chilled soup bowls and garnish with grapes and almonds.

CREAMED SHERRIED MUSHROOMS ON TOAST

Serves 4 to 6

A brilliant, classic combination, this dish has the earthiness of mushrooms infused with the nuttiness of sherry mellowed by cream. Lovely as it is on thick, trimmed slices of good toast, you can easily make it a little more elegant by serving in warm puff pastry shells. Choose excellent quality Oloroso to use in the dish and serve alongside.

2 lbs	assorted mushrooms, domestic and wild (brown cremini, chanterelles, cepes, trumpet), wiped clean, roughly chopped	1 kg
	juice of 1 lemon	
8 thick slices	home-style bread	8 thick slices
	olive oil for frying	
¼ lb	butter	125 g
1	large shallot, finely chopped	1
3 cloves	garlic, minced	3 cloves
	salt and freshly ground black pepper	
1 cup	Oloroso sherry	250 mL
1 cup	light cream	250 mL

1. Place the mushrooms in a colander and squeeze lemon juice over them. Leave to drain for 10 minutes or so.

2. Preheat oven to 400°F (200°C). Trim the crusts from the bread. In a large skillet, heat the oil and fry the bread until it is golden brown and crisp on both sides. Transfer it to a baking sheet and set aside.

3. In the same skillet, melt the butter over medium heat. Sauté the shallot and garlic until they are softened, about 5 minutes; do not brown. Add mushrooms to the pan, stir to blend and then season with salt and pepper. Add sherry, increase the heat and cook for 10 to 12 minutes until half the liquid is absorbed.

4. When reduced, add the cream and cook, covered, for another 5 minutes. Adjust seasoning, then distribute mushrooms evenly atop the reserved toast slices. Brown in the hot oven for 8 to 10 minutes and serve immediately.

PEI POTATO, BROCCOLI AND LEEK SOUP

Serves 6

A perfect choice to kick off a St. Patrick's Day dinner, owing to its pale green hue, this is a seriously good potato soup recipe and a slight variation on one devised by the PEI Potato Board. Serve a little of the sherry you choose to accompany the soup alongside in small creamers to be stirred into the soup at the table. Make sure to wash leeks thoroughly by slitting them open lengthwise and spreading them apart to rinse clean under cold water.

1 tbsp	olive oil	15 mL
3	leeks, trimmed, washed, sliced	3
1 clove	garlic, minced	1 clove
1	small onion, chopped	1
¼ cup	all-purpose flour	50 mL
3 cups	chicken broth	750 mL
3	PEI baking potatoes, peeled, cubed	3
2 cups	chopped fresh broccoli	500 mL
1 tbsp	chopped fresh thyme	15 mL
1 cup	milk	250 mL
1 cup	light cream	250 mL
	salt and freshly ground white pepper	

1. In a large saucepan, heat oil over medium heat. Add leeks, garlic and onion, and sauté, stirring occasionally, until vegetables are softened. Stir in flour and cook for 1 to 2 minutes, but do not allow flour to brown.
2. Add chicken broth, stirring constantly with a whisk to prevent lumps. Add potatoes, cover and reduce heat to a simmer. Simmer for 10 minutes, stirring now and then.
3. Add broccoli and thyme, and simmer for 10 to 15 minutes or until vegetables are tender.
4. Using a hand blender (or in small batches in a food processor or regular blender), purée soup until relatively smooth. Return to the saucepan over medium heat, and add milk and cream. Season to taste.
5. Do not allow to boil but simmer until heated through.

BISTRO-STYLE LENTIL SOUP

Serves 4 to 6

Here is a delightfully robust soup that elevates the humble lentil to new heights. This soup is almost a meal in itself, served with a selection of cheeses and warm, crusty bread. Serve the same Oloroso alongside that you use as an ingredient.

1-½ cups	dry lentils	375 mL
4 tbsp	unsalted butter	50 mL
4–5 slices	lean bacon	4–5 slices
1	onion, finely chopped	1
2 cloves	garlic, finely chopped	2 cloves
3-½ cups	chicken stock	875 mL
¼ cup	Oloroso sherry	50 mL
1	bay leaf	1
¼ lb	salt pork	125 g
½ cup	light cream	125 mL
2–3 slices	cooked ham, finely diced	2–3 slices
¼ cup	chopped parsley	50 mL
¼ cup	heavy cream	50 mL

1. Cover lentils with enough cold water to cover them by 2 inches (5 cm) and leave to soak overnight.

2. In a fairly deep, heavy saucepan, heat butter, add roughly chopped bacon and cook for 2 to 3 minutes. Add onion and garlic, and cook gently, being careful not to brown onion or garlic.

3. Drain the lentils and place them in pan; pour in chicken stock and sherry, and bring to a boil. Add bay leaf and salt pork. Cover and simmer gently until lentils are soft. Discard salt pork and purée mixture in a blender or food processor.

4. Return mixture to pan and stir in the light cream, ham and parsley. Warm a soup tureen and pour in the heavy cream. Pour hot soup slowly into a tureen and blend thoroughly. Serve immediately.

ALMOND CAKE

Serves 6

Serve this moist almond-infused cake with warm, unpeeled, toasted almonds and a dollop of crème fraîche. A springform pan makes it easier to remove the cake.

⅓ cup + 1 tbsp	butter, softened	75 mL + 15 mL
½ cup + 1 tbsp	all-purpose flour	125 mL + 15 mL
⅓ cup	extra virgin olive oil	75 mL
¾ cup	sugar	175 mL
¾ lb	marzipan (almond paste), softened, crumbled	375 g
	zest of 2 large lemons, finely grated	
5	eggs	5
1 tsp	baking powder	5 mL
¼–½ cup	sherry, sweet or dry	50-125 mL

1. Preheat oven to 325°F (160°C). Use 1 tbsp butter and 1 tbsp flour to butter and dust a 9-inch (23-cm) round cake pan or a springform pan. Line the bottom with parchment paper.

2. Using an electric mixer, beat the remaining butter, oil and sugar until they're light and fluffy. Add marzipan and lemon zest and beat until the mixture is smooth. With the mixer running, add the eggs one at a time. When the mixture is well blended and smooth, add the remaining flour and baking powder gradually and continue to mix.

3. Pour the batter into the pan and bake for 45 minutes or until a tester comes out clean. Remove pan from oven and let it cool in the pan.

4. When the cake has cooled but is still slightly warm, remove it from the pan and transfer it to a cake platter. Drizzle the sherry over top and serve warm.

PORT

Port is produced by stopping the fermentation of the grape must (juice) with grape brandy to leave residual sugar in the wine. The alcoholic strength varies from 20 to 22 per cent.

The tradition of drinking a glass of port after dinner has made us overlook its possibilities as an accompaniment to a meal or to be used in its preparation. Port, grown in Portugal's hot and savagely beautiful Douro Valley, is made from five preferred grape varieties: Touriga Nacional, Tinta Barroca, Touriga Francesa, Tinta Roiz (Spain's Tempranillo) and Tinta Cão.

The different designations of port can be confusing, but there are two basic types from which all the styles derive: Ruby (bottle aged) and Tawny (cask aged).

Ruby is deeply coloured, purple-ruby, with a sweet blackberry flavour. Young and rugged.

Tawny has a topaz colour and tastes nutty, raisiny with a hint of oxidation.

Aged Tawny is usually designated 10, 20, 30 or even 40 years old. Lighter in colour, drier, spicy dried fruit and nut flavour.

Vintage Port are the best wines of a declared vintage, bottled after two years and left for long aging. Rich, full-bodied, ripe blackberry and mulberry character, spicy and sweet. The wine will throw a heavy deposit over the years and will need decanting.

Single Quinta Vintage is a wine of a declared year from a specific farm (quinta), usually not as intense and concentrated as a vintage port that has been blended from several farms.

Colheita are tawny ports from a single year. The vintage date appears on the bottle.

LBV (Late Bottled Vintage) is a wine from a single year, bottled when it is between 4 and 6 years old. Not as rich and elegant as Vintage but a less expensive and worthwhile substitute.

Vintage character is a ruby port aged in cask and bottled after five years.

Crusted port is a wine from several vintages that leaves a deposit in the bottle, behaving like a vintage port.

BEST EXPRESSION

Taylor, Fonseca, Graham, Dow, Warre, Quinta do Noval, Ramos-Pinto, Sandeman, Niepoort

SUBSTITUTES

sweet sherry, Bual, Malmsey

White port is usually served as an aperitif either well chilled, on the rocks with a slice of lemon or with soda water. These wines, produced from such grape varieties as Gouveio, Malvasia Fina and Viosinho, are usually off-dry to medium sweet.

BEST EXPRESSION

Offley, Quinta do Noval

SUBSTITUTES

dry and medium-dry Vermouth

PEARS POACHED IN LBV WITH LEMON AND GINGER

Serves 4

Reserve this lovely sweet for a particularly special gathering. Serve with unsweetened whipped cream and simple biscotti. Zest the lemons before juicing them for this recipe.

4	firm pears of any variety	4
	juice of 2 lemons	
2-¼ cups	water	550 mL
2 cups	fine granulated sugar	500 mL
2	whole cinnamon sticks	2
6	cloves	6
2–3-inch piece	gingerroot	5–8-cm piece
	zest of 2 lemons	
⅓ bottle	Late Bottled Vintage port	⅓ bottle

1. Peel pears, keeping stem intact, and place them in a large bowl. Cover them with the lemon juice, turning them over a few times.

2. In a heavy-based saucepan, combine the water, sugar, cinnamon sticks, cloves, gingerroot and lemon zest. Stir to blend well, bring to a boil and simmer for 15 minutes.

3. Add the port, stir and let simmer for another 5 minutes. Add pears to this mixture. Cover with a sheet of waxed paper and place a plate on top to keep pears submerged in the port mixture. Simmer over a very low heat for about an hour, turning the pears occasionally to ensure even colouring, until they are tender. Remove pan from heat and let cool. Strain the port mixture into a measuring cup and discard spices.

4. Transfer pears to a serving bowl and pour the syrup over the pears. Refrigerate until chilled and serve as described above.

ERMITE BLUE CHEESE AND
WALNUT TART OLSON

Serves 6

This recipe is made to be served with a beautiful port, with its mixture of blue cheese, walnuts and dried cranberries. It is from Chef Michael Olson at On the Twenty in Niagara-on-the-Lake, the renowned dining room of Cave Spring Winery, who says: "This tart can be prepared in advance and served at room temperature, or served hot from the oven. Salt is not added to the recipe because of the salt content in the cheese."

For the pastry crust

1 cup	all-purpose flour	250 mL
½ tsp	salt	2 mL
½ cup	cold butter	125 mL
	ice water	

For the filling

½ cup	sour cream	125 mL
1	egg yolk	1
6 oz	Ermite blue cheese, crumbled	185 g
1 cup	coarsely chopped walnuts	250 mL
¼ cup	dried cranberries	50 mL
	pinch finely ground black pepper	

1. To make the pastry crust, in a mixing bowl combine the flour and salt. Cut in butter until mixture resembles coarse meal. Add just enough ice water to bring the mixture together in a ball. Wrap in plastic and chill for an hour.
2. Roll dough out onto a lightly floured board. Use it to line a 10-inch (25-cm) tart shell. Chill until firm, about 30 minutes. Preheat oven to 375°F (190°C).
3. Bake the tart shell for 12 minutes until it is golden brown around the edges. Remove it from oven; leave oven on.
4. To make the filling, in a mixing bowl whisk together the sour cream and egg yolk. Add cheese, walnuts, cranberries and pepper, and combine well. Pour into prebaked tart shell and bake 8 to 10 minutes, until cheese has melted and is beginning to brown.

CANTALOUPE WITH PROSCIUTTO AND PORT

Serves 6

Here is a twist on the favourite coupling of prosciutto and melon. In this variation, port lends a special quality to both the melon and the sweet, silky prosciutto. Cut the melons across their width, not length, so they serve as a vehicle for the port. Serve with warm, chewy bread sticks.

3	ripe cantaloupe melons, halved, seeded	3
6 cups	port	1.5 L
¾ lb	Italian prosciutto, sliced paper thin	375 g

1. Place each melon half in a shallow serving dish. Fill each one with a cup of port. Cover with plastic wrap and refrigerate for about an hour.
2. Just before serving, casually drape slices of prosciutto next to the cantaloupe. Serve immediately, with a couple of bread sticks at each serving.

ZABAGLIONE AL PORTO

Serves 4

A variation on the traditional Italian zabaglione based on Marsala, this version features the same simple ingredients—the freshest egg yolks and fine sugar—whisked together instead with Tawny port. Use this either as a dessert on its own or as a warm, sumptuous sauce for split, fresh figs. Sublime.

6	large egg yolks	6
6 tbsp	fine sugar	90 mL
⅔ cup	Tawny port	150 mL

1. Set a large pot of water on to boil. Once it is boiling, beat the egg yolks in a bowl (preferably stainless steel) with a whisk. When they are well blended, add the sugar and port, and whisk them together until foamy.
2. Set the bowl over the boiling water and continue to whisk vigorously until the custard foams up in the pan and becomes smooth and thick. Do not overcook. Serve at once.

CHAPTER 18

ICEWINE

Any grape that can hang on the vine until the mercury drops to a sustained temperature of 18°F (−8°C) can make Icewine. That's why you see such anomalies as Cabernet Franc Icewine. But the preferred grapes are Riesling and Vidal in Canada, sometimes Gewürztraminer and Chenin Blanc, varieties with thick enough skins to withstand some of the rigours of the winter. Icewine is produced from grapes left to freeze on the vine. The presses drive out the frozen water content, leaving about 20 per cent of the original juice. That juice is high in sugar and acid as a result of such concentration. The resulting wine is intensely sweet but also high in acidity, which balances the flavours.

TASTE PROFILE
A bouquet of honey, peach and apricot, with a caramel-like sweetness and tropical fruit flavours and a finish of sweet citrus fruits. The best will have a long, lingering finish.

BEST EXPRESSION
(Canada) Château des Charmes, Cave Spring, Inniskillin, Henry of Pelham, Vineland Estate, Stoney Ridge, Konzelmann; (Germany) Deinhard estates

SUBSTITUTES
Late Harvest Riesling, Sautèrnes, Barsac, Tokaji

GRILLED PEARS WITH VANILLA ICE CREAM

Serves 6

Nothing complements ice wine quite like warm pears. Serve this when fresh locally grown pears are at their peak. Choose any variety of firm, ripe pears for this recipe. Vary this recipe with ripe apricots!

6	ripe pears, halved, cored	6
1 cup	apricot nectar	250 mL
	quality vanilla ice cream as needed	
½ cup	warmed honey	125 mL

1. Preheat a lightly greased grill to medium high. Brush the pears generously on the cut surface with apricot nectar. Place on grill and cook, basting with the nectar and turning often, until pears begin to colour and become tender, about 5 to 8 minutes.

2. Transfer pears to serving plates. Add a scoop or two of vanilla ice cream to each plate and drizzle a little warmed honey over the pears and ice cream. Serve at once.

FRESH FIGS WITH HONEY RICOTTA

Serves 6

Elegant, easy and quick to assemble, this two-step dessert can be ready for guests in no time at all. Make the citrusy ricotta filling in advance and keep it refrigerated until the figs are ready to be filled. For different tastes, try brushing the figs with a little melted butter and grilling them.

12	ripe fresh black or green figs	12
1 cup	ricotta cheese	250 mL
1 tsp	finely chopped orange zest	5 mL
1 tsp	finely chopped lemon zest	5 mL
1 tsp	pure vanilla extract	5 mL
¼ cup	liquid honey	50 mL
¼ cup	slivered almonds	50 mL

1. Trim the stem end from each of the figs. Slice each fig into quarters, being careful not to cut through the blossom end entirely (the fig should be intact, in a shape resembling a tulip). Open each fig gently to form a cavity.
2. In a food processor or blender, combine the ricotta, orange and lemon zests, vanilla and honey. Process until the filling is relatively smooth. Use it to fill the cavity of each fig. Sprinkle figs with almonds and serve immediately.

APPLE AND ALMOND TART

Serves 6 to 8

Purchase good-quality frozen puff pastry for this dessert. You can make six or eight individual tarts instead of one large one, and you can use canned or fresh apricots in place of the apples. Serve with unsweetened whipped cream or vanilla ice cream.

½ pkg	frozen puff pastry, thawed	375 g
½ cup	ground almonds	125 mL
2–3	Granny Smith apples, peeled, cored, thinly sliced	2–3
3 tbsp	melted butter	45 mL
3 tbsp	sugar	45 mL

1. Roll out pastry until it is a very thin ⅛-inch (3-mm) shell, about 10 to 11 inches (25–28 cm) in diameter. Roll the pastry over the rolling pin and transfer it to a fluted tart shell. Use a fork to prick the pastry in a few places, then refrigerate for about 20 minutes.

2. Preheat oven to 425°F (220°C). Remove pastry shell from the refrigerator and sprinkle with almonds. Place apples in a concentric pattern in the pastry shell, ending with a few set within the centre. Brush or drizzle them with the melted butter and scatter the sugar over the surface.

3. Bake for 30 minutes until lightly golden brown.

SIENA CAKE

Serves 8 to 10

This flat, dense cake laden with dried fruits and nuts is a specialty of the Italian town of Siena. It is actually more of a confection than a cake. Because of its richness, you need only slice it in slivers. This makes a lovely gift.

¼ lb	shelled, blanched almonds	125 g
¼ lb	hazelnuts, lightly toasted	125 g
⅓ cup	cocoa powder	75 mL
1-½ tsp	cinnamon	7 mL
¼ tsp	allspice	1 mL
½ cup	cake and pastry flour	125 mL
¾ cup	candied orange peel, finely chopped	175 mL
¾ cup	candied citron, finely chopped	175 mL
¾ cup	candied lemon peel, finely chopped	175 mL
¾ cup	honey	175 mL
¾ cup	sugar	175 mL
2 tbsp	icing sugar	25 mL

1. In a mixing bowl, combine the almonds, hazelnuts, cocoa powder, cinnamon, allspice, flour, orange peel, citron peel and lemon peel, and mix to combine well.

2. In a large heavy-based saucepan, set over a low heat, combine the honey and sugar, and simmer, stirring constantly, until a candy thermometer registers around 240°F(115°C) and a bit of the mixture dropped into cold water forms a relatively firm ball.

3. Add the fruit and nut mixture to the saucepan and mix it thoroughly together. Preheat oven to 300°F (150°C).

4. Line a 9-inch (23-cm) springform pan with well-buttered parchment or waxed paper. Pour in the cake mixture, smoothing it out evenly with a metal spatula.

5. Bake for about half an hour. Remove it from the oven and let stand for a few minutes, until set. Remove the sides and bottom of the pan. After the cake has cooled somewhat, sprinkle it with icing sugar. Serve in thin slices.

INDEX

appetizers
    artichoke and cheddar squares, 76
    beef shank, braised, 105
    Brandade with Grilled Pita, 4
    cantaloupe with prosciutto and port, 167
    crab cakes, 9
    fritters, savoury, 71
    meatballs, 132
    mushrooms, grilled portobello, 97
    oysters, 7
    oysters, with chèvre and basil, 75
    oysters, with tomato compôte and parmesan crust, 131
    Pesto Crepes with Grilled Swordfish, 56
    salmon salad, with tomato vinaigrette, 12
    scallops, Provençal, with endive, 80
    swordfish rolls, stuffed, 8
apple, and almond tart, 172
apricot chutney, 60
artichoke, and cheddar squares, 76

bacon, cheese, and potato cake, 117
bean, cannellini, and roasted garlic salad, 77
beef
    Bollito Misto with Salsa Verde, 90
    brisket, 90
    English Cottage Pie, 88
    London broil, 151
    meatballs, 132
    prime rib, roasted, 115
    shank, braised, 105
    steaks with mustard cream, 94
    tenderloin, 122
    tournedos, with mustard and onion sauce, 116
Bollito Misto with Salsa Verde, 90
Brandade with Grilled Pita, 4
bread pudding, chocolate, 154
broccoli, potato and leek soup, 160

cabbage, salmon, and leeks, 16
cakes
    almond, 162
    lemon loaf, 38
    Siena, 173
cantaloupe, with prosciutto and port, 167
cheese, bacon and potato cake, 117
chick peas, sausage and, 139
chicken
    breasts, with tomato basil vinaigrette, 50
    breasts, with truffle and fontina, 102
    Guinea Hen Korma, 32
    lime ginger, with salsa, 30
    livers (Sambal Goreng), 65
    livers, with sherry and shallots, 157
    Paella, 140
    with red peppers and roasted garlic, 83
    Shahi, 26
    tarragon, with cream, 79
    Thai, with basil and red peppers, 36

chowder, Sweet Corn and Pepper Chowder, 3
chutney, apricot, 60
clams, Paella, 140
cod
    Brandade with Grilled Pita, 4
    Provençal, 52
corn, and pepper chowder, 3
crab, and honeydew melon salad, 68
crab cakes, 9
crepes, pesto, with grilled swordfish, 56
curry
    Guinea Hen Korma, 32
    haddock in curry cream, 29
    lamb, with apricots, 37

desserts
    almond cake, 162
    apple and almond tart, 172
    bread pudding, chocolate, 154
    figs, 171
    lemon loaf cake, 38
    pears, grilled, 170
    pears, poached, 165
    Siena Cake, 173
    Zabaglione al Porto, 168
duck
    barbecued, pasta, 152
    ragout, 112

Eggplant Parmigiana, 135
eggs
    frittata, and Swiss chard, 47
    Huevos Rancheros, 46
    quiche, with Gruyère and ham, 78
    Zabaglione al Porto, 168
English Cottage Pie, 88

fava beans, linguine and, 87
fennel, bucatini, and tomato, 133
fettuccine, scallops and, 18
figs, with honey ricotta, 171
fish
    bouillabaisse, Spanish, 48
    Brandade with Grilled Pita, 4
    Cod Provençal, 52
    haddock in curry cream, 29
    halibut, pistachio crusted, 15
    Kedgeree, 43
    salmon salad, with tomato vinaigrette, 12
    salmon with cabbage and leeks, 16
    salmon, smoked, and leeks with tagliolini, 28
    salmon, smoked, and sorrel soup, 6
    swordfish rolls, stuffed, 8
    swordfish, with pesto crepes, 56
    tuna, grilled citrus, 64
Frittata with Swiss Chard and Pancetta, 47
fritters, savoury, 71
Fritto Misto, 19
fruit
    apple and almond tart, 172
    cantaloupe with prosciutto and port, 167
    honeydew, and crab salad, 68

pears, grilled, 170
pears, poached, 165

haddock
    in curry cream, 29
    Kedgeree, 43
halibut, pistachio crusted, 15
ham, Paella, 140
Huevos Rancheros, 46

Kedgeree, 43

lamb
    curry with apricots, 37
    Moussaka, 92
    with red wine and rosemary, 143
    shanks, with parsnips, 142
    stew with olives, 150
    tenderloins, 110
leek, potato and broccoli soup, 160
lemon, loaf cake, 38
lentil soup, 106, 161
linguine, with fava beans, 87
liver, calf, with caramelized onions, 118
lobster, Paella, 140
London Broil, Grilled, 151

macaroni, baked with cauliflower, 10
meat
    beef brisket, 90
    beef shank, braised, 105
    beef tenderloin, 122
    beef tournedos, 116
    Bollito Misto with Salsa Verde, 90
    calf liver with caramelized onions, 118
    English Cottage Pie, 88
    Hunter's Rabbit, 121
    lamb shanks, with parsnips, 142
    lamb stew with olives, 150
    lamb tenderloins, 110
    lamb with red wine and rosemary, 143
    London broil, grilled, 151
    meatballs, 132
    Moussaka, 92
    Osso Buco Alla Milanese, 126
    oxtails in Tempranillo, 144
    pork chops, stuffed, 100
    pork loin, 99
    pork tenderloin, five-spice orange, 63
    pork tenderloin, with watercress, 25
    pork, sage and garlic, 60
    prime rib, roasted, 115
    sausage and chick peas, 139
    sausage and rapini, 149
    sausages and onions in red wine, 89
    sparerib stew, spicy, 86
    steak on ciabatta, with Stilton butter and frisée, 84
    steaks with mustard cream, 94
    Torta Rustica, 124
    tourtière, with red onion confit, 108
    veal chops, with peach salsa, 59
    venison, 107

meatballs, Polpette di Carne, 132
melon, honeydew, and crab salad, 68
Moussaka, 92
mushroom salad, 20
mushrooms
    penne, and tomatoes, 134
    portobello, grilled, 97
    and sausage risotto, 98
    sherried, on toast, 159
    soup, cream of wild, 55
mussels
    Paella, 140
    soup, with cream and garlic, 58

noodles, Szechwan spicy, 35

onion
    confit, red, 109
    and sausages, in red wine, 89
    tart, 45
orzo, with black olives, sun-dried tomatoes and chèvre, 74
Osso Buco Alla Milanese, 126
oxtails, in Tempranillo, 144
oysters
    with chèvre and basil, 75
    salt and pepper, 7
    with tomato compôte and parmesan crust, 131

Paella, 140
pancakes, potato, with back bacon, chèvre and McIntosh
        apples, 24
pasta
    barbecued duck, 152
    bucatini, with fennel and tomato, 133
    fettuccine and scallops, 18
    linguine with fava beans, 87
    macaroni, baked with cauliflower, 10
    orzo, with black olives, sun-dried tomatoes and
        chèvre, 74
    penne with mushrooms and tomatoes, 134
    salmon, smoked, and leeks with tagliolini, 28
    Szechwan spicy noodles, 35
    toasted, with scallops and smoked salmon, 23
    Torta Rustica, 124
peach, salsa, 59
pears
    grilled, 170
    poached, 165
penne, with mushrooms and tomatoes, 134
peppers, corn and, chowder, 3
Pesto Crepes with Grilled Swordfish, 56
pizza, prosciutto, 153
pork
    chops, stuffed, 100
    loin, 99
    meatballs, 132
    roast, sage and garlic, 60
    tenderloin, five-spice orange, 63
    tenderloin, with watercress, 25
    tourtière, with red onion confit, 108
potato
    cake, cheese and bacon, 117

pancakes, with back bacon, chèvre and McIntosh
     apples, 24
soup, broccoli and leek, 160

quiche, with Gruyère and ham, 78

rabbit, hunter's, 121
rapini, and sausage, 149
rice
     Paella, 140
     Porcini and Sausage Risotto, 98
     risotto, with squash, 44
risotto
     butternut squash, 44
     mushrooms and sausage, 98

salad
     cannellini bean and roasted garlic, 77
     crab and honeydew melon salad, 68
     mushroom, with Parmigiano Reggiano, 20
     mushrooms, grilled portobello, 97
     salmon, with tomato vinaigrette, 12
salmon
     salad, with tomato vinaigrette, 12
     smoked, and leeks with tagliolini, 28
     smoked, and scallops, with toasted pasta, 23
     smoked, and sorrel soup, 6
     with cabbage and leeks, 16
salsa
     cruda, 66
     fresh, 30
     peach, 59
     Salsa Verde, 91
Sambal Goreng, 65
sandwich, steak, with Stilton butter and frisée, 84
sausage
     and chick peas, 139
     and onions in red wine, 89
     and rapini, 149
     Torta Rustica, 124
scallops
     and fettuccine, 18
     Provençal, with endive, 80
     and smoked salmon, with toasted pasta, 23
seafood
     crab and honeydew melon salad, 68
     crab cakes, 9
     Fritto Misto, 19
     Mussel Soup with Cream and Garlic, 58
     oysters, 7
     oysters, with chèvre and basil, 75
     oysters, with tomato compôte and parmesan crust, 131
     Paella, 140
     scallops and fettuccine, 18
     scallops and smoked salmon, with toasted pasta, 23
     scallops, Provençal, with endive, 80
shrimp, Paella, 140
Siena Cake, 173
soup
     Ajo Blanco Barrenechea, 158
     bouillabaisse, Spanish, 48
     lentil, 106, 161

mushroom, wild, 55
mussel, with cream and garlic, 58
potato, broccoli and leek, 160
sorrel and smoked salmon, 6
Sweet Corn and Pepper Chowder, 3
spareribs, spicy stew, 86
squash, risotto, 44
steak
     on ciabatta, with Stilton butter and frisée, 84
     with mustard cream, 94
Sweet Corn and Pepper Chowder, 3
swordfish
     grilled, with pesto crepes, 56
     rolls, stuffed, 8

tart
     apple and almond, 172
     blue cheese and walnut, 166
     onion, 45
tomatoes
     and fennel, with bucatini, 133
     Huevos Rancheros, 46
     penne and mushrooms, 134
     roast, gratin, 136
Torta Rustica, 124
tourtière, with red onion confit, 108
tuna, grilled citrus, 64
turkey, tostadas, 66

veal
     chops with peach salsa, 59
     Osso Buco Alla Milanese, 126
     tourtière, with red onion confit, 108
vegetable terrine with mozzarella, 72
vegetables
     beef tenderloin, with winter vegetables, 122
     cabbage and leeks with salmon, 16
     cauliflower, with baked macaroni, 10
     cheese, bacon and potato cake, 117
     corn and pepper chowder, 3
     Eggplant Parmigiana, 135
     fava beans, with linguine, 87
     fennel and tomato, with bucatini, 133
     mushroom salad, 20
     mushroom soup, 55
     mushrooms, grilled portobello, 97
     mushrooms, sherried, on toast, 159
     onion confit, red, 109
     onion tart, 45
     onions, and sausages, in red wine, 89
     potato pancakes, with back bacon, chèvre and McIntosh
          apples, 24
     rapini and sausage, 149
     sorrel soup with smoked salmon, 6
     squash risotto, 44
     Swiss chard, frittata, 47
     terrine with mozzarella, 72
     tomato gratin, 136
venison, 107

Zabaglione al Porto, 168